MOTORCYCLE
OWNER'S
MANUAL

MOTORCYCLE
OWNER'S
MANUAL

HUGO WILSON

A DK PUBLISHING BOOK

Editor
David T. Walton

Senior editor
Louise Candlish

US editors
Leah Kennedy, Laaren Brown

Photographer
Andy Crawford

Managing editor
Sean Moore

Art editor
Sasha Kennedy

Senior art editor
Tracy Hambleton-Miles

DTP designers
Zirrinia Austin, Mark Bracey

Production
Kate Hayward

Deputy art director
Tina Vaughan

First American Edition, 1997
10 9

Published in the United States by DK Publishing, Inc.,
375 Hudson Street, New York, New York 10014
Visit us on the World Wide Web at http://www.dk.com

Copyright © 1997 Dorling Kindersley Limited, London
Text copyright © 1997 Hugo Wilson

Library of Congress Cataloging-in-Publication Data

Wilson, Hugo
    Motorcycle owner's manual / by Hugo Wilson. -- 1st American ed.
      p. cm.
    Includes index
    ISBN-13: 978-0-7894-1615-5
    ISBN-10: 0-7894-1615-8
      1.Motorcycles--Maintenance and repair--Handbooks, manuals, etc.
    I. Title.
    TL444.W55 1996
    629.28'775--dc20
                                  96-35925
                                  CIP

Reproduced by
C. H. Colour Scan, Malaysia
Printed and bound in China
by WKT Company Ltd.

IMPORTANT NOTICE
Use this book in conjunction
with your owner's manual
and the shop manual
appropriate to your machine.

Contents

Introduction.................. 6
Motorcycle anatomy...................... 8

Basics.......................... 14
Control comfort.......................... 16
Free play adjustment.................... 17
Level checks and fill-ups............. 18
Lights, bulbs, and fuses................ 20
Bulb access................................. 22
Battery maintenance.................... 23
Drive chain................................. 24
Wheel removal............................ 26
Loose bolts and leaks.................. 28
Tire check.................................. 29
Suspension explained................... 30
Suspension adjustment................. 32
Bodywork removal....................... 34
Cleaning..................................... 36

Simple service jobs....... 38
Lubrication explained.................. 40
Oil and oil filter change.............. 42
Gearbox oil................................. 44
Air filter..................................... 45
Fuel system checkup and clean.... 46
Spark plugs................................. 47
Brakes explained.......................... 48
Brakes check and change............. 50
Hydraulic fluid............................ 52
Cable lubrication........................ 53
Transmission explained............... 54

Chain and sprocket replacement.. 56
Wheel alignment.......................... 58
Steering and suspension 60

More complex tasks...... 62
Four-strokes explained................. 64
Four-stroke maintenance.............. 67
Changing the camshaft belt.......... 69
Two-strokes explained.................. 70
Two-stroke components............... 72
Ignition explained....................... 74
Timing checks and adjustment..... 76
Carburetors explained................. 78
Carburetor maintenance............. 80
Clutches explained....................... 82
Clutch maintenance..................... 84
Suspension problems................... 86
Front fork overhaul..................... 88

The unexpected............ 90
Electrical systems........................ 92
Electrical problems...................... 94
Starting problems........................ 96
Tire and tube removal................. 98
Nuts and bolts............................ 100
Accident damage......................... 101

MAINTENANCE CHART.................. 102
GLOSSARY................................... 104
INDEX 108
ACKNOWLEDGMENTS................... 112

Introduction

YOUR MOTORCYCLE IS A SOPHISTICATED machine that requires regular maintenance and periodic repair to keep it running at its best. Despite the apparent complexity of the modern machine, even an inexperienced mechanic can carry out some maintenance tasks; if you can rewire a plug, you can work on your bike. Don't feel overwhelmed, but don't start a job unless you understand what is involved. Start by cleaning your bike and performing simple maintenance tasks. As your experience and your toolkit expand, you can move on to basic servicing, followed by more complex jobs. Some jobs, like carburetor balancing and tappet adjustment, require special tools or some experience and may be best left to a professional. Whatever level you're working at, the rules are the same: work in clean and neat conditions on a clean and

neat bike with the best tools you can afford. Keep your owner's manual and shop manual handy to help you with machine-specific details. Be methodical, don't rush, and, when you finish the job, double-check that you have correctly replaced and retightened all the parts concerned. A well-maintained bike is safer, more economical, and more satisfying to ride. And if you've fixed it yourself, it will feel even better.

Motorcycle anatomy

INDIVIDUAL MOTORCYCLISTS have different requirements from their bikes. To satisfy different types of riders and conditions, manufacturers produce machines with a huge variety of capacities, performance, and specification. But although a scooter may look very different from a "superbike," they both operate using similar systems and principles. Additionally, parts that require regular maintenance, adjustment, inspection, or replacement are common to most machines.

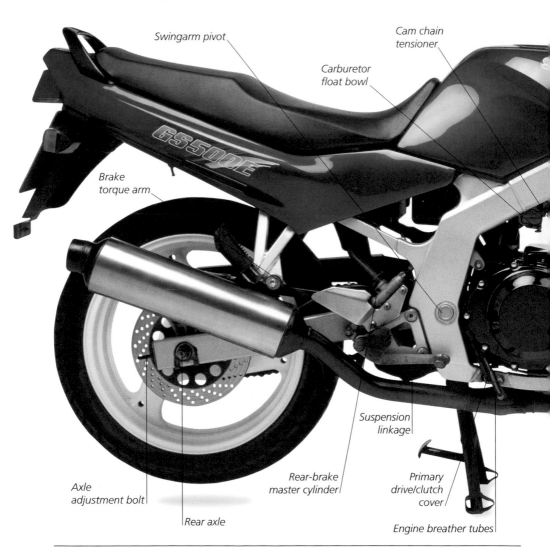

Swingarm pivot

Cam chain tensioner

Carburetor float bowl

Brake torque arm

Suspension linkage

Axle adjustment bolt

Rear axle

Rear-brake master cylinder

Primary drive/clutch cover

Engine breather tubes

Brake fluid reservoir

Gear lever

Fuel tap

Instrument housing

Tachometer drive

Speedometer drive

Rear sprocket

MIDDLEWEIGHT MACHINES

This is a typical middleweight machine featuring an air-cooled, twin-cylinder, four-stroke engine that drives the rear wheel via a six-speed gearbox and chain final drive. Suspension is provided by telescopic forks at the front and a rising-rate linkage and single suspension unit at the rear. Disc brakes are fitted to the front and rear wheels.

Bottom yoke

Fork tube

Camshaft cover

Cotter pin

Engine oil filler cap

Front axle

Other types of motorcycles

SPORTS BIKE

Designed for optimum performance and handling, sports bikes use modern technology to full effect. Because of their exceptional performance, these bikes demand to be kept in peak condition, but their complex engines, suspension, braking, and control systems can make maintenance an intimidating prospect for home mechanics. However, high design and manufacturing standards mean that servicing is surprisingly infrequent and can often be done by competent home mechanics with no special tools.

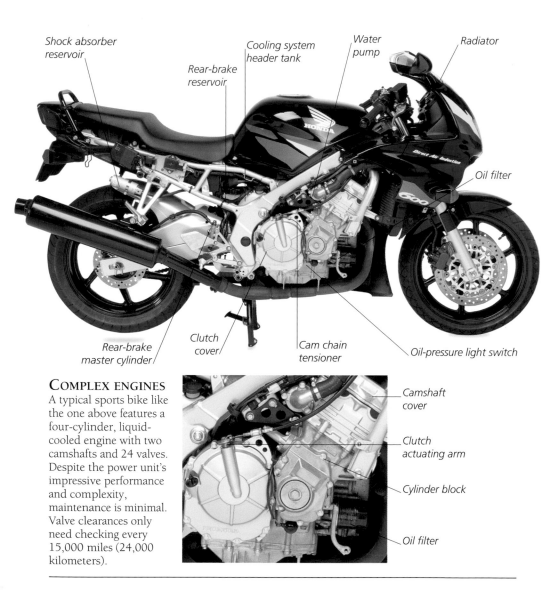

Shock absorber reservoir

Cooling system header tank

Water pump

Radiator

Rear-brake reservoir

Oil filter

Rear-brake master cylinder

Clutch cover

Cam chain tensioner

Oil-pressure light switch

COMPLEX ENGINES

A typical sports bike like the one above features a four-cylinder, liquid-cooled engine with two camshafts and 24 valves. Despite the power unit's impressive performance and complexity, maintenance is minimal. Valve clearances only need checking every 15,000 miles (24,000 kilometers).

Camshaft cover

Clutch actuating arm

Cylinder block

Oil filter

TRAIL BIKE

The simple and rugged construction of trail bikes makes them ideal for novice riders and mechanics. They are easy to ride, simple to maintain, and straightforward to repair. Their construction is orthodox, and they rarely feature unusual or complex design details. In common with other lightweight motorcycles, single-cylinder two-stroke engines are popular on small-capacity trail bikes. In this case, the engine is liquid cooled and the chassis components are conventional. More utilitarian lightweights may use drum brakes and twin-shock rear suspension systems rather than the disc brakes and linkage-operated rear suspension system shown here.

Reed valve block

Box-section swingarm

Two-stroke oil tank

Headlight housing

Fork gaitor

Rocker arm

Floating caliper

Suspension link

THE TWO-STROKE

In its most basic form, the two-stroke engine has only three moving parts, but its operation is a complex process involving severe design compromise. Regular maintenance is minimal, but life span – especially of high-performance machines – can be much shorter than a comparable four-stroke.

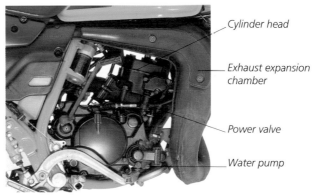

Cylinder head

Exhaust expansion chamber

Power valve

Water pump

CUSTOM BIKE

Designed for looks rather than performance, custom bikes use uncomplicated components. The engines rarely have more than two cylinders and are often in the classic V-twin formation. The rear suspension often features the old-fashioned twin-shock arrangement, and low-maintenance shaft- or belt-final-drive systems are also popular. Low power outputs, design simplicity, and ease of access make these bikes attractive to home mechanics.

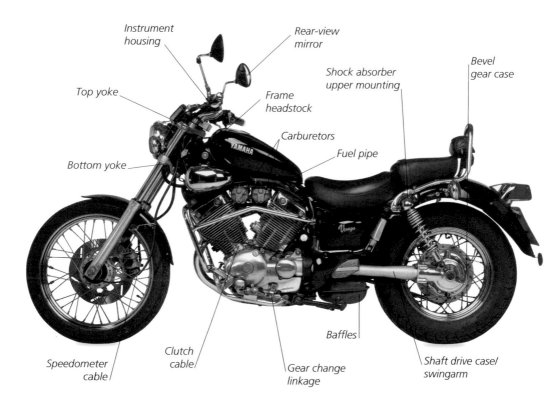

Instrument housing

Rear-view mirror

Shock absorber upper mounting

Bevel gear case

Top yoke

Frame headstock

Carburetors

Fuel pipe

Bottom yoke

Speedometer cable

Clutch cable

Gear change linkage

Baffles

Shaft drive case/ swingarm

AIR COOLING

Simpler and older four-stroke engine designs often rely on air cooling. Engines with a modest power output do not require the precise temperature control offered by liquid cooling. Air-cooled engines may also have fewer valves, camshafts, and other complexities than liquid-cooled engines.

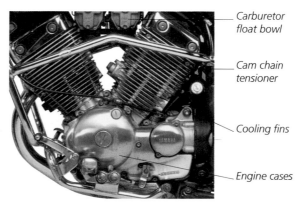

Carburetor float bowl

Cam chain tensioner

Cooling fins

Engine cases

SCOOTER

A typical modern scooter is made with a small-capacity two- or four-stroke engine and constantly variable transmission system. The suspension often incorporates a pivoting engine assembly at the rear and trailing- or leading-link forks at the front. Fully enclosed bodywork not only protects the rider but conceals a pressed-steel frame. Scooters are simple, user-friendly machines that require little maintenance.

Rear-brake lever

Fold-up seat

Brake caliper

Inspection cover

Trailing-link fork

Speedometer cable

Rear-brake cable

Cast-alloy wheel

AUTOMATIC TRANSMISSION

Scooters and mopeds have automatic transmission systems, making them simple to ride. A variety of systems are in use. The type shown here has a variable pulley/belt to offer an almost infinitely variable gear ratio. The system's moving parts are hidden behind a metal casing.

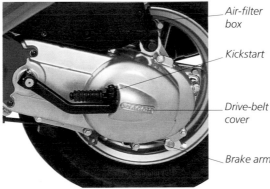

Air-filter box

Kickstart

Drive-belt cover

Brake arm

Basics

EVERY FIVE HUNDRED MILES, or once a week, you should give your machine – whether it is a "superbike" or a scooter – a thorough inspection and do any necessary adjustment or lubrication. These tasks can be performed by anyone with the most fundamental DIY (do-it-yourself) knowledge; if you can rewire a plug you should be able to do the basic checking and maintenance tasks on your bike. Details of these jobs are included in this section, as are instructions on how to undertake other essential tasks. Cleaning your bike will help maintain its value and encourages you to do a thorough inspection of the machine. Removing bodywork and cycle parts is sometimes necessary before other jobs can be undertaken – for example, if you get a puncture, the wheel will have to be removed before it can be fixed. Adjustment of suspension and the controls allows you optimum machine control and comfort.

WHAT YOU WILL NEED
The toolkit supplied with your motorcycle should be adequate for performing the jobs described in this "Basics" section, although better quality tools are preferable. For specific information relating to your machine, you will also need the manual supplied by the manufacturer. Other items, such as lubricants, a tire-pressure gauge, and cleaning products, may also be required for some jobs.

Shown here is a typical example of a standard toolkit. Yours may contain different items specific to your bike.

Pressure gauge
Buy a good tire-pressure gauge and keep it clean and safe.

Feeler gauge
Used for checking clearance on brakes when fitting the front wheel.

Allen wrench
This 5mm Allen wrench must be turned by using a spanner wrench.

Pliers
A basic, cheap pair of pliers is adequate for simple jobs.

Open-ended spanner wrenches
These tools have different sizes at each end.

BE YOUR OWN MECHANIC

These tasks and checks in the "Basics" section will help to keep your motorcycle operating efficiently and safely between regular servicing and reduce your reliance on professional mechanics. As you gain in mechanical confidence and interest, you can progress to the "Simple service jobs" section.

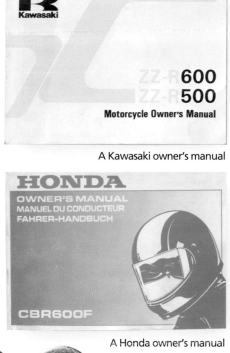

A Kawasaki owner's manual

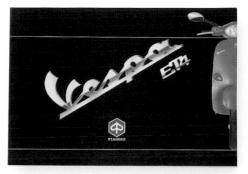

A Honda owner's manual

Owner's manuals
Containing a wealth of critical information, your owner's manual should be read before you work on your bike

Screwdriver with interchangeable ends
A shared handle can be used with a range of different-sized screwdrivers.

Extension bar and ring spanner wrenches
Adding the extension onto the end of the ring wrench will give you extra leverage for stubborn nuts. Make sure it doesn't slip.

Pin or "C" spanner wrench
This tool is used for adjusting the shock absorber. It is possible to use the extension bar for extra leverage.

Control comfort

PEOPLE COME IN a greater range of shapes and sizes than motorcycles, and many modern machines have adjustable brake and clutch levers with variable spans for different hand sizes. Rear-brake- and gear-pedal angles can also be altered to suit different riders. In order to achieve optimum handling control of the motorcycle, the rider should take full advantage of these features.

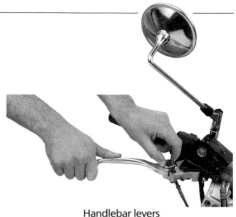

Handlebar levers
Many modern bikes have adjustable-span levers for the front brake and clutch. A numbered dial on the lever offers four different settings.

REAR-BRAKE-PEDAL ANGLE

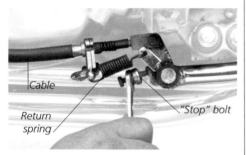

Cable

Return spring

"Stop" bolt

DRUM BRAKE
The brake-pedal angle is dictated by a movable "stop," usually controlled by a bolt. There may be a locknut that must be loosened before the bolt is turned. Reset the free play afterward.

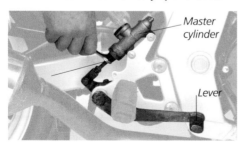

Master cylinder

Lever

DISC BRAKE
The pedal angle on a bike with a hydraulic rear disc brake is adjusted by altering the rod length between the lever and the master cylinder. Undo the locknuts and turn the rod's sleeve.

GEAR LEVERS

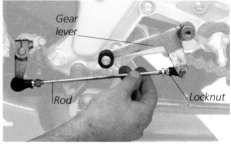

Gear lever

Rod

Locknut

GEARS WITH AN OPERATING LINKAGE
The gear lever on many machines is moved by adjusting the length of the linkage rod that connects the pedal to the gearbox shaft. Undo the locknuts and twist the rod to alter its length.

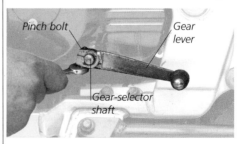

Pinch bolt

Gear lever

Gear-selector shaft

DIRECTLY FITTED LEVERS
If the gear lever is fitted directly to the gear-selector shaft, its position can be changed as follows: remove the pinch bolt, slide the lever off the shaft, reposition it, and secure it.

Free play adjustment

As CABLES STRETCH, AND BRAKE and clutch components wear, the amount of free play in the controls will alter and the levers must travel farther in order to activate the brake or clutch. Cables are fitted with a screw adjuster at one or both ends to alter the amount of available free play. As well as handlebar controls, cables may also be used to operate some rear brakes.

BRAKE LEVER ADJUSTMENT

Correct free play
is usually
2–3mm

Locknut

Screw
adjuster

Cable

1 TURN THE SCREW ADJUSTER
To remove excessive free play, the outer part of the cable must, effectively, be lengthened. This is done by using the screw adjuster, which is found at one or the other end of the cable, to reduce the amount of inner cable available. Loosen the locknut, then turn the screw adjuster until the free play is reduced to the correct amount; in handlebar levers, this is usually about 2–3mm (⅒in).

2 DON'T OVERTIGHTEN
Always make sure that you do not overtighten any cables because this can cause brakes to bind, clutches to slip, or engine idle speeds to increase. Because the handlebars move in relation to the components operated by the handlebar controls, it is essential to have some free play. If the controls become stiff or "notchy" during operation, the cables should be disconnected and lubricated (see p.53).

ROD-OPERATED REAR BRAKES

Free play adjustment in rod-operated rear brakes is achieved by shortening the length of the rod. This is done using a simple screw adjuster. However, you must make sure that there is still enough free play remaining so that the brake does not operate in response to the suspension being compressed. After adjusting the brake, always check that the brake light is operating correctly.

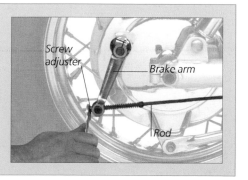

Screw
adjuster

Brake arm

Rod

Level checks and fill-ups

To keep your bike operating safely and efficiently, the correct quantity of fluids must be maintained in the bike's cooling, lubrication, and hydraulic systems. Oil, coolant, and hydraulics levels should be checked regularly and refilled when necessary. Fluid reservoirs and tanks are fitted with sight windows or easy-to-use dipsticks to allow simple checking of the levels. If your bike's consumption of these fluids is excessive, it may indicate that there is a problem; check the system for leaks. The level of the acid in the battery should also be checked (see p.23).

OIL CHECK

Maximum level mark

Minimum level mark

Dipstick

DIPSTICK

The dipstick sits in the filling port of either the oil tank or the engine. To check the oil level, the bike should be level and, ideally, the engine cold so that all the oil has settled in the sump or tank. The dipstick must be removed and wiped clean before being returned to its correct position (see your owner's manual). It can then be removed and inspected for an accurate reading.

Sight window | Crankcase

SIGHT WINDOW

The alternative to a dipstick is a sight window in the crankcase. This has marks to indicate the upper and lower levels.

FOUR-STROKE OIL SUPPLY

In the four-stroke recirculating lubrication system, oil is pumped around the engine to various moving parts before returning to the engine sump or a tank. If not replaced regularly, the oil will become worn out and contaminated. Check the oil level in the sump or tank between services and refill when necessary.

TWO-STROKE OIL SUPPLY

Two-strokes use a "total-loss" lubrication system: oil is burned in the engine with the fuel and can't be reused. Check the level regularly and refill when necessary with two-stroke oil. Most modern two-strokes have a separate lubrication system as well as a low-level warning light.

Two-stroke oil

HYDRAULICS SUPPLY

Hydraulic brakes and clutches are self-adjusting. Fluid from the reservoir is taken into the system to compensate for brake- or clutch-component wear. Check the reservoir level regularly and refill if necessary. If the brake system's fluid level drops markedly, check for brake pad wear – and, if necessary, replace the pads – *before* filling the reservoir. Drain and replace the fluid every two to three years.

Brake fluid

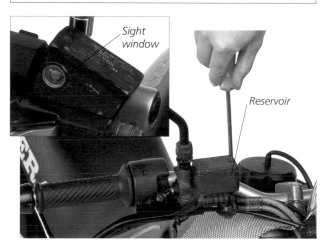

Sight window

Reservoir

1 CHECK BRAKE FLUID

Brake fluid is corrosive and toxic so be careful not to spill it. Hydraulic fluid reservoirs are either translucent or have a sight window. With the bike on even ground, check that the fluid is between the upper and lower lines. Unscrew the reservoir cap (on circular reservoirs, this will be a screw-on type).

2 ADD BRAKE FLUID

Remove the diaphragm beneath the cap to expose the fluid. Because hydraulic fluid is hydroscopic – absorbs water from the atmosphere – always use fluid from a fresh container. Also, be sure that it is compatible with the fluid already in the system. After adding sufficient fluid, replace the diaphragm and the cap.

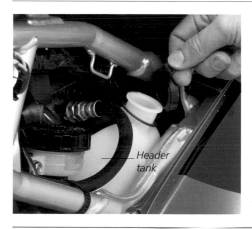

Header tank

COOLANT SUPPLY

Most liquid-cooled bikes have a transparent header tank with the minimum and maximum levels for the coolant marked. Pay attention to the level. When filling up the tank, use the correct water and antifreeze mix (this is usually 50/50 but check your owner's manual) or a premixed coolant, and make sure it is the same type as that already in the machine. Another function of antifreeze is to inhibit corrosion, thus helping to protect the cooling system. If liquid loss is significant, check the cooling system for leaks and loose hoses. A leaking cylinder head gasket will also affect fluid levels.

Lights, bulbs, and fuses

As PART OF YOUR REGULAR motorcycle checkup you should be sure that all lights and electrical components are working. Light failure is usually due to blown bulbs. Although bulbs are easily replaced, access to them can be awkward, especially to instrument illumination and warning light bulbs. Consult your owner's manual for specific information.

BULBS AND THEIR LOCATIONS

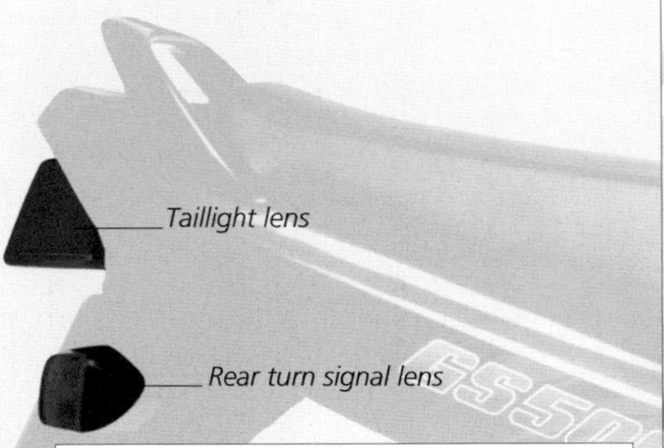

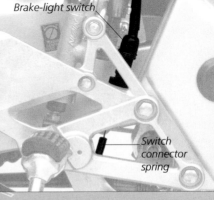

Brake-light switch

Switch connector spring

Taillight lens

Rear turn signal lens

Combined stop- and taillight bulb	Bayonet-fitting bulb	Wedge-fitting bulb

BRAKE-LIGHT SWITCHES

As brake-lining material wears, the pedal position moves. Adjust the collar on the switch so the bulb lights when the pedal is pressed. The switch is connected to the brake lever with a spring. Check switch operation before replacing a suspected blown bulb. Switches operated by hydraulic pressure, which are often used on front brakes, should be maintenance free.

BULB TYPES

Bulbs differ according to volt/watt specifications and fitting types. Sidelights and instrument housings use small bayonet- or wedge-fitting bulbs. Turn signals use a bayonet fitting. Stop- and taillights are combined in a two-filament bulb with a bayonet fitting. It usually has offset fitting pins so that it can't be fit incorrectly.

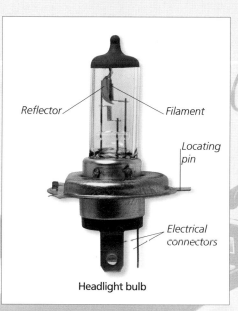

Reflector

Filament

Locating pin

Electrical connectors

Headlight bulb

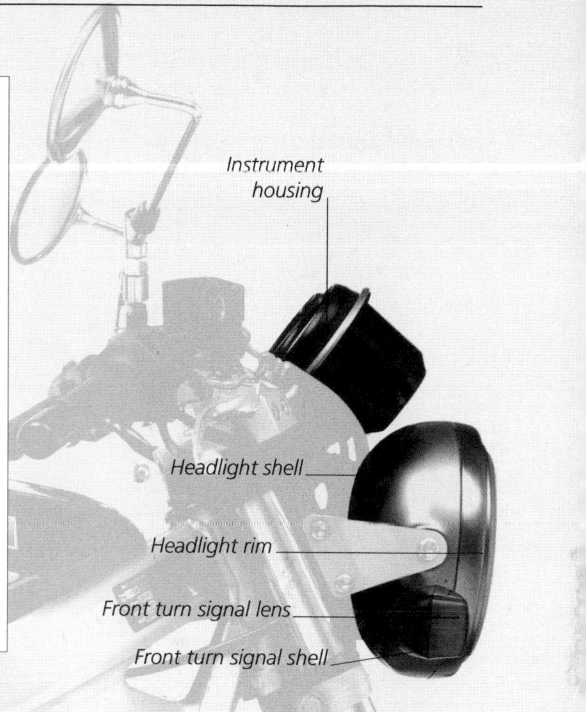

Instrument housing

Headlight shell

Headlight rim

Front turn signal lens

Front turn signal shell

LOW AND HIGH BEAM

A headlight bulb has two filaments – one for high beam and one for low – and is usually held in place with a spring clip. It is connected to the electrical system via a three pronged connector. As always, replace a broken bulb with one of the same specification. It is good practice not to touch the glass of a bulb, especially a halogen one, since this reduces its lifespan. Volt and watt specifications vary between machines.

Ceramic fuses

Blade fuse

Glass-cartridge fuse

TYPES OF FUSES

A fuse is a safety feature that blows if an electrical circuit overloads in order to prevent damage either to the circuit or its components. The system – or that part of it covered by the fuse – then fails. A fuse should blow only if the system is faulty, but freak failures can occur. Replace the fuse with one of the correct amp rating, and if that blows too, trace the system fault. Fuse locations vary, and your bike may use one or more of any of the fuses pictured.

Bulb access

ACCESS TO A MOTORCYCLE'S light bulbs can be awkward, so you may need
to consult your owner's manual. Bulbs are hidden behind a lens, and access
is gained either by removing the lens to reach the front of the bulb or by
removing the holder that contains the bulb through the rear of the unit.

REMOVING AND REPLACING BULBS

1 UNSCREW THE RIM
To gain access to
the headlight bulb on an
unfaired motorcycle, you
must first remove the lens.
This is usually attached to a
metal rim, which is, in turn,
screwed to the headlight
shell. Remove the screws.

2 REMOVE THE BULB
Once unscrewed, the
lens/reflector unit can be
pulled away. Always take
care to support it during
the disassembly process.
After pulling off the plug,
the spring clip can be seen;
take it off and the bulb can
then be removed.

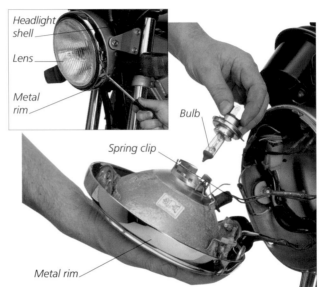

Headlight shell

Lens

Metal rim

Bulb

Spring clip

Metal rim

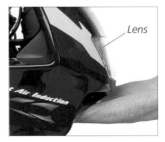

Lens

Bulb holder

FAIRED HEADLIGHTS
On faired bikes, the lens/
reflector unit remains in place,
and the bulb is withdrawn
from the rear. Access must be
gained from behind the fairing
or below, as shown here. The
connectors and fitting may be
protected by a rubber sheath.

TURN SIGNAL LENSES
The lenses for turn signal
bulbs are either screw-on, as
shown here, or push-fit types.
To remove push-fits, pry
gently with a screwdriver,
avoiding any damage to the
lens. Turn signal bulbs have
bayonet fittings.

REAR-LIGHT BULBS
Most rear-light bulbs have
two filaments, for stop and
taillights, and sometimes, two
two bulbs are used. Access is
gained either via a screw-on
lens or, as shown here, through
the back of the unit. Be careful
not to lose any screws.

Battery maintenance

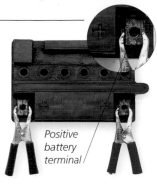

MOST MOTORCYCLES have conventional lead/acid batteries, which should have their fluid levels checked weekly. If used for short trips with the lights on, the battery may need occasional recharging. Well-maintained batteries should last a long time, but the need for frequent fill-ups or charging may mean that you're due for a replacement. Some bikes have maintenance-free batteries, which benefit from a short charge with a special "float charger." Never try to open or add fluid to a maintenance-free battery.

Positive battery terminal

Connecting the battery charger
To recharge, remove the battery's plugs and connect the charger's black clip to the negative terminal and the red clip to the positive.

FILLING UP AND RECHARGING THE BATTERY

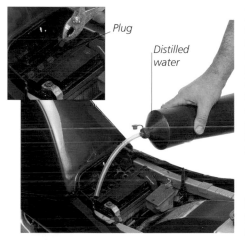

Plug

Distilled water

BEFORE YOU START
Check the battery's fluid level using the markings on the side of its case. If it is below the minimum mark, the battery must be filled up. It is sometimes easier to remove the battery from the machine before refilling or recharging it. You should only use deionized or distilled water to fill up the battery level; never use acid to fill up a used battery. If your battery requires regular refilling, it may mean that the electrical system is overcharging.

1 FILL UP THE FLUID
Remove the plugs from the top of the battery; they may be push-in or screw-in types. When filling up the fluid level, keep in mind that it should cover the battery plates.

Battery lead

2 CHARGE THE BATTERY
Disconnect the battery leads, negative first. It is a good idea to make a note of the polarities in order to reconnect them correctly. If necessary, unstrap the battery before removal. Keep the battery upright to avoid spills. Charge at a third of the battery's ampere hour (Ah) rating to avoid overcharging (see top).

3 RECONNECT THE BATTERY
Clean the terminals with steel wool, reconnect the battery, and smear the terminals with petroleum jelly – this helps to prevent corrosion. Make sure that the terminals are tight and that the battery is securely set in place.

Drive chain

THE MOST COMMON FORM of transferring power from gearbox to rear wheel is the drive chain. It is compact, simple, and efficient. To keep it in good condition, regularly (at least once a week, but certainly before a long ride) lubricate, adjust, and inspect it for rust, damaged rollers, and loose pins. To tighten the chain tension, move the rear wheel away from the gearbox sprocket; this process varies between bikes, so check your owner's manual for the correct chain tension. If your bike has a single-sided swingarm, its rear axle is mounted on an eccentric; rotating this alters the axle's position. The eccentric, which is held in position by a cotter pin, can be turned with a large "C"-spanner wrench. Maintenance prolongs chain and sprocket life, but replacement is inevitable and expensive.

CHECKING, ADJUSTING, AND LUBRICATING

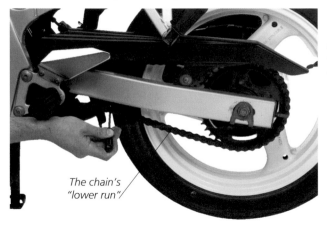

The chain's "lower run"

1 CHECK TENSION
The chain tension should be checked on its lower run. The tension may vary so check at more than one point. If the chain is tighter or looser at different points, it has a "tight spot." Adjust the tension to the correct setting at the chain's tightest spot. If the tight spot is severe, replace the chain. If the chain has worn so it no longer fits snugly onto the sprocket teeth, replace it. If adjustment is unnecessary, go to Step 4.

2 LOOSEN AXLE NUTS
Some motorcycles have a security pin, which will need to be removed before you can loosen the axle nuts. You may find that the axle nuts are very tight. If so, the spanner wrench supplied with your bike may not be long enough to give adequate leverage. If this is the case, it may be worth investing in a more suitable one. Bikes with a single-sided swingarm require a slightly different technique (see above).

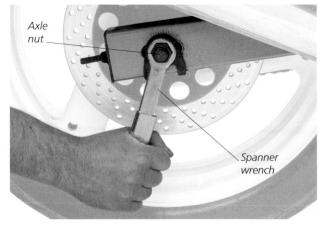

Axle nut

Spanner wrench

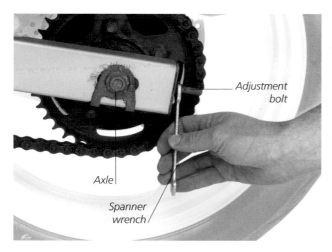

Adjustment bolt

Axle

Spanner wrench

3 MOVE THE AXLE
In order not to disturb wheel alignment, you must move the axle back by the same amount on each side of the wheel. If your bike's chain-adjustment bolts have locknuts, loosen these first. Then turn the adjustment bolts by either a quarter-turn or a sixth of a turn at a time. Check the tension after moving both bolts. Retighten the axle nuts, and then recheck the tension before tightening the locknuts and replacing security pins. Don't overtighten the chain.

4 LUBRICATE
Aim the spray lubricant at the inside of the chain while rotating the wheel to give an even coating. On bikes with O-ring chains, which have grease sealed into the rollers, extra "lubing" only protects its exterior. Some lubricants can destroy an O-ring chain's seals. Beware: excess lubricant leaves a sticky mess on the rear wheel and tire.

Spray lubricant

Spray along the lower run

REGULAR MAINTENANCE

CLEAN WITH A BRUSH
Periodically cleaning the chain with kerosene or diesel on a soft brush will enhance chain life.

WIPE WITH A CLOTH
With a cloth, wipe the chain dry and apply fresh lubricant. For more details on chains and sprockets see pp.54–57.

Wheel removal

YOU CANNOT REMOVE a wheel unless the bike is firmly supported and the wheel is clear of the ground. Few bikes have stands that allow the removal of either wheel – most lift only the rear wheel off the ground, but the front one can be raised by placing a jack or blocks under the engine. If the bike has no center stand, ideally bike stands should be used. If no stands are available, the bike must be supported by other means. Be careful not to strain your back, and only begin work when the bike is secure; if it can fall, it will.

THE REAR WHEEL

Most motorcycles require slightly different wheel removal techniques, and it is impossible to cover them all here. The example below is typical of a bike with a rear disc brake and an endless chain.

THE FRONT WHEEL

On drum-brake machines, it may be necessary to disconnect the brake cable, torque arm, and speedometer cable before withdrawing the wheel. On disc-brake machines, you may have to take one or both of the brake calipers off before it is possible to remove the wheel. The techniques vary from bike to bike.

REAR WHEEL REMOVAL

1 REMOVE THE BOLT

Undo the axle nuts and gently tap the axle through the swingarm with a soft-faced mallet. The nut may be held by a spring clip or split pin; remove this before undoing the nut. Once the axle has been pushed from one side, you should be able to pull it clear through the wheel. This may be difficult if the chain is tight; if this is the case, loosen the axle adjustment bolts, being careful to move each bolt by an equal amount.

Split pin

2 REMOVE THE WHEEL

Remove the axle's spacers, noting the order as you do so, and push the wheel forward. Unhook the chain from the sprocket and move it from the wheel. This task may be eased by removing the chain guard. Withdraw the wheel while supporting the brake caliper, but don't allow it to hang by its hose. Reassemble by reversing the process.

FRONT WHEEL REMOVAL

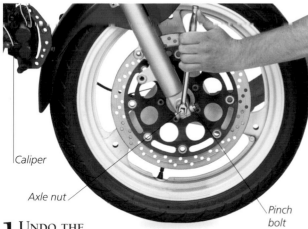

Caliper

Axle nut

Pinch bolt

1 UNDO THE AXLE NUT

Remove any drum brake connections or, if necessary, remove one or both calipers. Do not allow the calipers to hang by their hoses, but support them with string. Now undo the axle nut.

Speedo-meter cable

Fork leg

Spacer

2 REMOVE THE WHEEL

Loosen the security bolts that pass through the fork leg. Support the wheel and withdraw the axle. Remove any spacers and then pull the wheel free. Make sure that you make a note of the location of the spacers so that they are replaced in the correct order.

VARIATIONS

• It is usual to remove a drum-brake rear wheel with the unit in place. Before removing the axle and spacers, disconnect the brake cable or rod, and, if fitted, detach the torque arm from the brake.

• "Quickly detachable" (QD) rear hubs on some bikes allow wheel removal without chain disturbance. Undo and remove the axle, spacers, and any drum-brake-related fittings, and pull the wheel clear of the cush-drive rubber. This will remain on the sprocket carrier attached to the swingarm.

• On shaft-drive bikes, the procedure is similar to removing a QD wheel. Disconnect brake cables and torque arms, then remove the axle and spacers. Pull the wheel clear of the gear housing.

• Single-sided swingarms make rear-wheel removal easy. The wheel is held in place by one large nut or several small ones. Remove these and slide the wheel off the axle assembly. The wheel nut may have a retaining clip, which must be replaced on reassembly.

• Some machines – mainly scooters – also have single-sided front suspension. Loosen the bolt(s) and remove the wheel from the axle.

Loose bolts and leaks

VIBRATION AND WEAR can cause fluid-carrying components to leak, bolts to undo, and clips to fall off. You should make a regular inspection of your bike to make sure that nothing is about to fall off or empty its contents. The ideal time to do this inspection is when you are cleaning the bike. Don't forget to check for damage to wheels and other components at the same time.

NUTS, BOLTS, AND CLIPS

Be aware of rattles and other strange noises. Wiggle and prod components to make sure that they are securely held in place. Tighten any loose bolts and nuts.

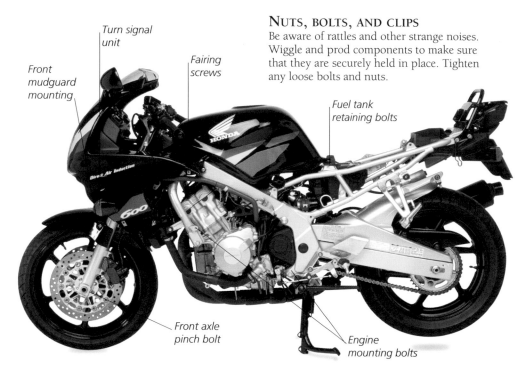

Turn signal unit

Front mudguard mounting

Fairing screws

Fuel tank retaining bolts

Front axle pinch bolt

Engine mounting bolts

CHECKING FOR LEAKS

There are several fluid-carrying components on your bike. Leaks of vital fluids can damage your bike or even be dangerous. You should inspect the following areas carefully:

• For signs of leaking hydraulic fluid: brake-fluid reservoirs, brake calipers, hydraulic lines.
• For signs of gas leaks: fuel lines, fuel taps, fuel tanks, carburetors.
• For signs of oil leaks: oil filters, oil coolers, external oil lines, engine drain plugs.
• For signs of suspension-fluid leaks: shock absorbers, forks.
• For signs of coolant leaks: radiator hoses, radiator, header tank.

Broken spoke

WHEEL INSPECTION

It is good practice to inspect your wheels regularly. In particular, you should look for any damage to the wheel rim, and check that none of the spokes are broken.

Tire check

THE TIRES ON YOUR MOTORCYCLE are the critical link between the bike and the road. If they are not in good condition and correctly inflated and mounted, the performance and handling of the bike will be severely impaired. Incorrect inflation and mounting can be potentially dangerous, and possibly fatal.

PRETRIP TIRE CHECK

Pressure gauge

1 CHECK PRESSURE
Your regular tire check should include making sure that the tires are inflated to the correct pressure. Buy a good-quality tire-pressure gauge and use it regularly. With use, tires warm up, and this affects their pressure. Therefore, for an accurate reading you should always check the pressure before riding the machine.

2 INFLATE TIRES
If necessary, add air using a foot pump or a compressed-air line. Always recheck the pressure using your own gauge rather than the gauge on the pump or air line. It is a good idea to check the accuracy of your gauge periodically by comparing it with the gauge at your local tire store.

Foot pump

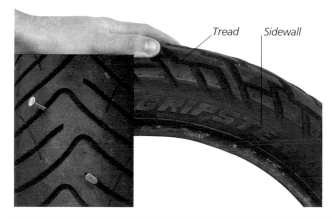

Tread   *Sidewall*

3 CHECK TREAD DEPTH
Inspect your tires for cracks, cuts, and irregular swellings. Remove any object that is embedded in the tread. Check that your tires meet the legal requirements for minimum tread depth. It is said that 90 percent of tire failures occur within the last 10 percent of the tire's life. Badly worn tires will also impair the machine's handling. If tires are badly damaged, they should be replaced.

Suspension explained

SUSPENSION INSULATES THE RIDER and the machine from bumps in the road and also keeps the wheels on the ground. If the wheels are airborne they cannot transmit power, braking, or steering forces. Suspension is provided by a combination of springs and dampers. The spring isolates the main part of the machine from the wheels, and the dampers control the speeds at which the spring compresses and rebounds. The relationship between the two functions is critical to the machine's good handling.

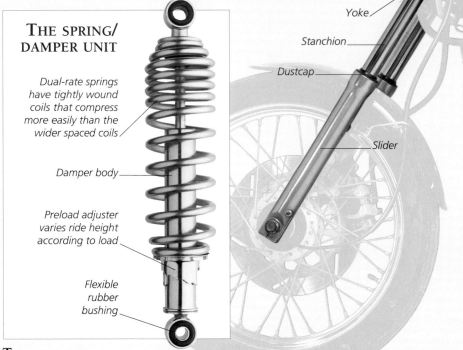

THE SPRING/
DAMPER UNIT

Dual-rate springs
have tightly wound
coils that compress
more easily than the
wider spaced coils

Damper body

Preload adjuster
varies ride height
according to load

Flexible
rubber
bushing

Yoke

Stanchion

Dustcap

Slider

THE PRELOAD

Springs are designed to be a specific height and to compress under a specified load. If the spring does not compress easily enough, it will transfer shocks to the machine and rider. If too easily compressed, its movement will be used too quickly; it will bottom out and again transfer shocks to the machine and rider. Rising- or dual-rate springs offer a compromise: the farther they are compressed, the more force is required to compress them. This gives a comfortable ride without the risk of excessive bottoming. Ideally, different springs should be used for different loads but, in reality, this isn't possible. However, some adjustment is provided by varying the spring's "preload": increasing it means that more force is needed to start compressing the spring. This compensates for increased load at the expense of reduced suspension travel.

CROSS SECTION OF A SPRING/ DAMPER UNIT

Suspension should compress easily at first, to absorb small bumps, then progressively harden to prevent bottoming out

The volume or type of gas affects the springs' compression rate

A small amount of compressible gas in the chamber allows for the displacement of the incoming rod

Nonreturn valves allow varying speeds of compression and rebound damping

Hydraulic fluid chamber

ONE-WAY VALVES

Dampers work by restricting the flow of oil through passages within the suspension unit. As the unit is compressed or extended, oil is displaced by a piston. It is forced through holes containing one-way valves to provide different rates of compression and rebound damping. The damping rate is controlled by the size and number of holes as well as the viscosity of the oil. Using a heavier grade of oil will increase the damping, while using a lighter oil will have the reverse effect. It is important that any suspension unit be sealed so that the oil, and any gas that the design incorporates, cannot escape.

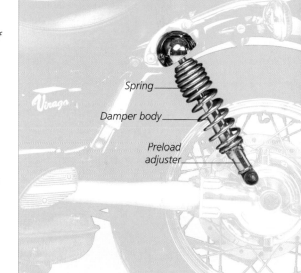

Spring

Damper body

Preload adjuster

FRONT SUSPENSION

On almost all motorcycles, the front suspension is provided by telescopic forks, in which the spring and the damper are incorporated in the fork leg. The wheel is mounted at the bottom of the fork legs, and the forks are also used to transfer steering forces. On scooters, a leading- or trailing-link system is more common. These have removable suspension units similar to those used on the rear of most machines.

THE SWINGARM

Rear suspension is provided by mounting the wheel at one end of a fork (swingarm), which pivots from the frame at its other end. The fork's movement is controlled by suspension units that combine the spring and the damper. Simple designs use one unit on each side of the wheel. In more complex versions, a single suspension unit is operated from the swingarm via a linkage, which provides a rising-rate effect.

Suspension adjustment

ALL BUT THE MOST BASIC bikes offer some suspension adjustment. Variations in spring preload and damping allow comfort and handling to suit different riders and conditions. But while correct suspension adjustment can improve the feel of your machine, incorrect adjustment can make it worse. All alterations mean compromise: improving one area may worsen another. If you can't feel the difference, use the manufacturer's recommended settings.

PRELOAD ADJUSTMENT

The load on the rear suspension will alter greatly according to whether a pillion or luggage is being carried. Additional load will cause the suspension to sag and bottom out easily. Increasing the preload on the spring restores the ride height of the bike to normal. To adjust the preload, you must turn the cam that holds the spring to the damper body. The cam is in the form of a notched spiral collar.

SINGLE-UNIT SYSTEMS

Adjustment of single-unit systems is achieved in the same way as one of a pair of units, by turning a collar on the damper body. This must usually be done using a special "C" spanner wrench. As the collar is turned, the spring is compressed or extended. Compressing the spring increases the preload. On single-unit systems, access is often exceptionally awkward. This makes adjustment tricky as well as time consuming.

FRONT FORK PRELOAD

Even if a pillion passenger and extra luggage are carried, variations in load will not be as significant on the front of the bike as at the rear. For this reason, the facility for adjusting the front fork preload is not a universal feature and is mainly offered on high-performance machines. On the bike shown here, the adjustment is provided by using a spanner wrench to turn the caps on the top of the fork to one of four possible positions.

Cap

Top of the fork leg

DAMPING ADJUSTMENT

Compression damping controls the speed at which the spring compresses when it hits a bump. Rebound damping controls the time that it takes to return to its original state. Consult your owner's manual to find out what adjustments are provided on your machine, where the adjusters are located, and what the manufacturer's recommended settings are. Most screw adjusters increase the damping effect as they are turned clockwise. As they are turned, the adjusters will click into different positions. Here, the rebound damping on the front forks is adjusted by screws on top of the fork legs.

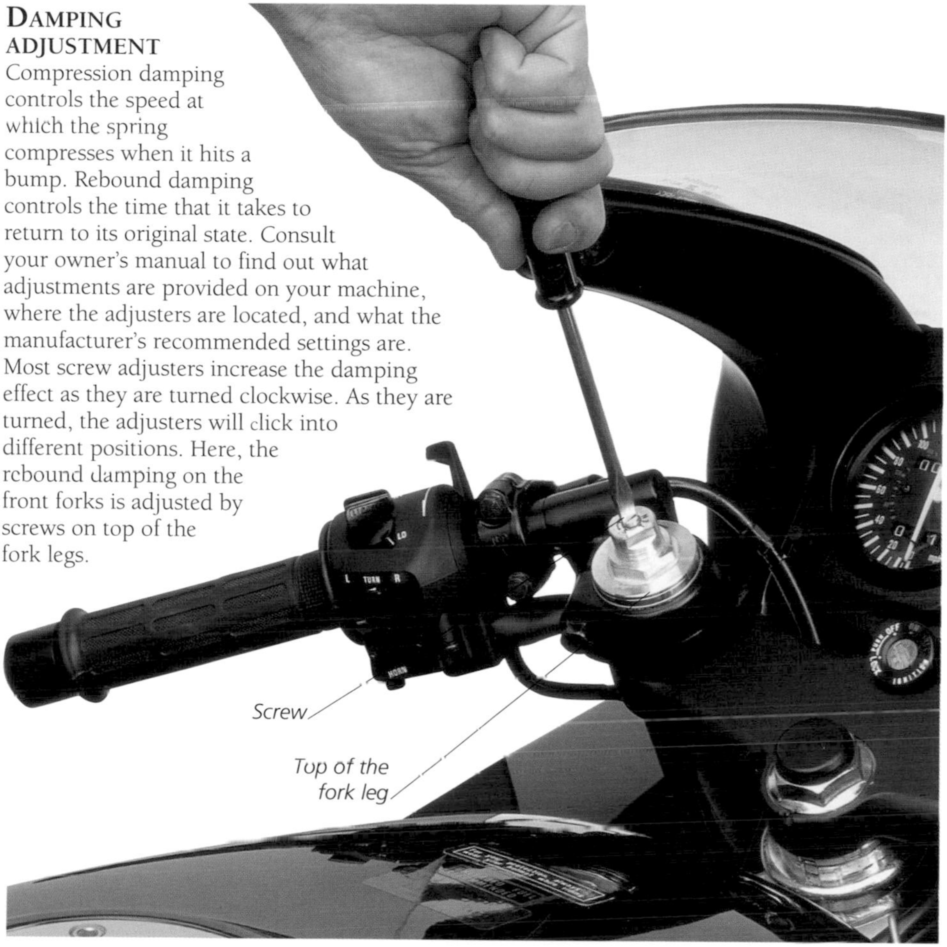

Screw

Top of the
fork leg

REAR DAMPING

This bike's rear suspension has adjustable compression and rebound damping. The rebound is adjusted by a screw in the damper body, while compression is adjusted by a screw on the remote reservoir (left). Damping adjustment is very easy to mess up. Experiment with it, but if it doesn't feel any better, return to the recommended settings, which should offer a reasonable compromise.

Bodywork removal

MODERN MOTORCYCLES are increasingly fitted with fairings and other body panels that impair access to their working parts. These are held in place by a variety of fasteners – clips, tags, screws, and bolts – and often must be removed for maintenance. Consult your owner's manual for bodywork removal details. Body parts are expensive and damage easily: paintwork chips and scratches, and plastics get scratched and cracked. Even small defects detract from your bike's appearance, so place anything that you remove safely out of the way where it won't get knocked or kicked, ideally on some clean, soft material.

Seat
Fuel tank
Access panel
Lower panel
Complete fairing
Side panel

REMOVING THE BODYWORK

Mounting lugs

Side panel

SIDE PANEL REMOVAL
Usually, side panels are either a push-fit type or have an obvious, easily operated catch or screw. You should never use excessive force when removing or replacing push-fit panels; the mounting lugs are often fragile and damage easily. Simply give a firm but gentle tug as close to the mounting lugs as possible. When replacing panels, make sure that any lugs are correctly located before pushing the panel firmly into place.

ACCESS PANEL REMOVAL
Some faired machines have access panels that allow limited access to some engine parts without necessitating the removal of the entire fairing. In the example shown here, the panel is retained with two Allen-head screws and lugs, and access gained is to the spark plugs. As with all types of panels, make sure that you ease it back into place as gently as possible. If you discover that any screws are missing on any panel, replace them immediately because vibrations created by loose fittings can cause panels to crack.

FAIRING-LOWER REMOVAL

Large panels can be awkward to remove and replace. Lightly tape the panels in place while removing the fasteners. After replacement, make sure that lugs and guides are correctly located before tightening the fasteners.

SEAT REMOVAL

Some bikes have a hinged seat, secured by a lock or catch. Release the catch and lift the seat up. The seat shown here is secured at the rear by bolts. Undo the bolts, then pull the seat back and upward to clear the front hook-type fitting.

Gas tank

FUEL TANK REMOVAL

Although fuel tank removal is rarely necessary for simple maintenance, you may need to remove it for more serious tasks. Fuel lines should be disconnected. Some bikes have wiring connected to the tank; this must also be disconnected. The tank is often secured at the front by rubber grommets on the frame that push into slots in the tank. The rear of the tank is secured with bolts or a strap. After undoing the strap or loosening the bolts, gently pull the tank backward and lift it clear of the frame.

STRIPPED-OFF BODYWORK

For most basic maintenance jobs, removing the top part of the fairing is not usually necessary. For work on the front wheel, brakes, or forks, it may be necessary to remove the front fender – this is usually quite straightforward. When replacing body parts, make sure that all lugs and guides are located correctly before tightening fasteners. It may be useful to protect or locate body parts with tape during refitting.

Cleaning

REGULARLY CLEANING YOUR MOTORCYCLE will help keep it in top condition. In addition to washing away road dust, dirt, and oil, you should try to prevent corrosion and rust by using polish, wax, and water-repellent spray on unprotected surfaces. Corrosion can quickly tarnish chrome and metal, while wear and tear on paintwork can be made worse by moisture. The cleaning process not only maintains the appearance of your machine but also allows you to inspect it thoroughly, thereby locating loose fasteners, fluid leaks, and other problems at an early stage.

CLEANING STEPS

Wash with soapy solution

Rinse with clean water

Soft brush

1 DEGREASE
Approach the job methodically, starting at one end of the bike and working toward the other. Apply a degreasant with a soft brush to the parts that attract oily dirt: rear wheels, suspension linkages, and engines are all susceptible. Hard brushes can scratch your paintwork and damage plastic finishes.

2 SOAP AND RINSE
Wash off the degreasant using a low-salt detergent. (Normal household detergent has a high alkali content and will encourage corrosion.) Use a soft sponge or cloth to apply the soapy solution. Wash the machine thoroughly with clean water afterward to remove all degreasant and detergent. Wipe dry with a chamois cloth.

3 LUBRICATE AND POLISH
After cleaning the bike, make sure that all unprotected surfaces are coated in water-repellent spray or sparingly applied light oil. The chain, pivot points, and other exposed moving parts should be relubricated. Unprotected metal, especially on wheels, must be polished regularly to prevent rusting, as should chrome and other bright metal. Protect the paintwork by waxing it.

TOOLS FOR CLEANING

Sponge

Bucket

Chamois

Soft
brush

Cloth

Shampoo and polish
Special detergents with a low
alkali content are ideal for
washing your motorcycle.

*Wipe the
bodywork dry*

*Polish the
paintwork*

PREWINTER CARE

Bikes that are used in
winter conditions should
be kept well lubricated
and be regularly washed to
prevent corrosion. Protect
or polish exposed metal,
apply grease to exposed
bolts and threads, keep the
chain and all cables well
lubricated, and protect
electrical connections
with marine grease or
petroleum jelly. If the
bike is to be stored for
the winter, it should
be clean and dry
and have new oil
in the engine.
Disconnect the
battery, oil the chain
and other exposed
moving parts, and
drain the carburetor
of fuel by running the
engine with the fuel tap
turned off until the bike
stops. The fuel tank
should also be drained.
Finally, push the brake
pads back from the discs,
and store the bike under
a blanket in a dry place.

POWER WASHER

Effortless, thorough cleaning can be achieved with a power
washer, but use it carefully because it can remove paint and
stickers and damage vulnerable bike parts. Protect bearings,
chains, carburetors, and electrical connections. Some
spray-can chemicals are corrosive, so rinse thoroughly.

Simple service jobs

MOST MACHINES REQUIRE BASIC SERVICING every 3,000–4,000 miles (5,000–6,500 kilometers), some more frequently, others less. For most modern bikes, this is usually a series of simple inspections and adjustments (and an engine oil change for four-strokes), none of which is beyond a sharp, amateur mechanic, although you'll need higher-standard tools than those supplied with your bike (see below). Wash the bike, and work methodically and thoroughly in a clean, well-lit environment, making sure you have everything you need nearby.

TOOLS AND TIPS

Do not damage your bike. Use the right tool for the job and use it properly. Tools should fit snugly onto fasteners, and if a fastener will not undo, there is a reason. Avoid using excessive force, and make sure that you are following the correct procedure as outlined in your manual.

Allen wrenches
Many fasteners have Allen heads. Use good-quality wrenches to prevent damage and breakages.

Chain link breaker
This tool may help when removing or shortening chains. If possible, borrow one.

Shop manual
For the most accurate information, use a manual specific to your bike. Factory manuals are best but they are expensive.

Combination spanner wrenches
These are ideal for most jobs. Use the ring end if access allows since it provides a better grip on the nut.

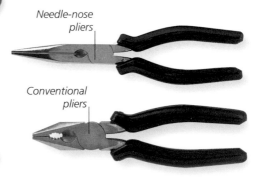

Needle-nose pliers

Conventional pliers

Pliers
Both needle-nose and conventional pliers are essential in your motorcycle's toolkit.

Spark plug gauge and adjuster
This cheap and simple tool makes checking and adjusting gaps easy.

Lubrication tool
This simple tool will help prolong cable life.

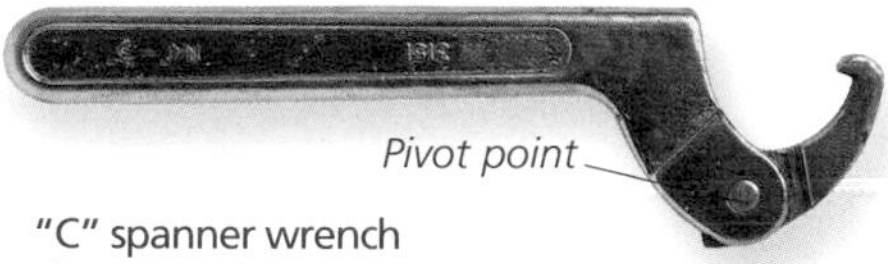

Pivot point

"C" spanner wrench
These wrenches are required on some bikes for exhaust nuts and other applications, such as shock absorber adjustment.

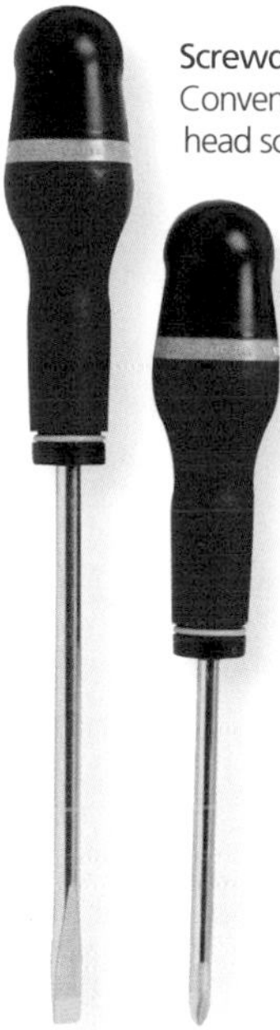

Screwdrivers
Conventional and Phillips-head screws come in several sizes. You should always use a good-quality screwdriver of the correct size and type.

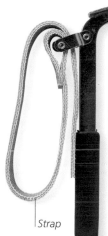

Strap wrench
Ideal for removing spin-on oil filters, a strap wrench makes oil changes easier.

Strap

Mallet
Sometimes you will have to hit things. When you do so, use a soft-faced mallet to avoid damaging the component.

Grease gun
If your bike has grease fittings, you will regularly need to use a grease gun on them.

Socket set
This is an essential part of the toolkit, so buy the best you can afford. A ⅜-inch drive set including 8-, 10-, 11-, 12-, 13-, 14-, 17-, 19-, and 22mm sockets is ideal for most jobs.

Lubrication explained

ALMOST EVERYWHERE THAT TWO PARTS move while in contact with each other, there is a need for lubrication. The point of lubrication is to reduce friction and wear, improve the action, and dissipate heat and dirt. Different applications require very different types of lubricant.

OIL EXPLAINED

Different engines operating in different conditions need different types of oil, the viscosity of which, denoted by its SAE (Society of Automotive Engineers) number, is critical. The higher the SAE number, the greater the oil's viscosity. Modern four-strokes need multigrade oils, which contain additives that allow the oil to operate at a range of viscosities depending on conditions. An SAE 10W/40 oil behaves like an SAE 10W at low temperatures, but as engine temperature increases, it adopts the characteristics of an SAE 40 lubricant. Thus, optimum lubrication occurs under both cold and hot conditions.

An oil's quality is indicated by its API (American Petroleum Institute) grade, shown by two letters. On gas engine lubricants, the first letter is "S." The following letter ranges from "A" (low quality) to "H" (high quality). As the lubricant quality improves, so the last letter progresses. Most bike manufacturers specify SE, SF, or SG engine oil. If a manufacturer specifies a 10W/40 API SE oil, any motorcycle oil from a reputable oil company that meets those specifications should be acceptable. Synthetic oils are claimed to give superior performance to conventional oils, but they are more expensive.

FOUR-STROKE LUBRICATION

Four-stroke engines use a recirculating lubrication system. The oil is stored in a tank or sump, from which it is pumped to the engine's moving parts. After use, it returns to the sump by gravity. Four-stroke engine oil and its filters should be changed regularly (see pp.42–43).

TWO-STROKE ENGINE OIL

Because two-stroke engine oil is burned during the combustion process, it needs to be very different from four-stroke oil. The quality of the oil is critical in high-performance machines, and you should only use the manufacturer's recommended lubricant. For more basic machines, any good-quality two-stroke oil designed for motorcycles should be adequate.

WET- AND DRY-SUMP ENGINES

In four-strokes, if the oil is stored in the sump of the engine, it is called a wet-sump engine. If there is a separate tank to which the oil is pumped from the sump, it is called a dry-sump engine.

GEARBOX AND DRIVE SHAFT OIL (TRANSMISSION FLUID)

The oil used in the gearbox and the drive shaft has a much easier job than engine oil. It is a simpler lubricant and needs changing less frequently. You should use the manufacturer's specified grade, usually a single-grade gear oil. The viscosity of gear oils is not numbered in the same way as that of engine oils.

LUBRICATION POINTS

The figures given below are approximate. If you travel particularly long distances, you should lubricate all your bike's parts more regularly.

(1) The wheel bearings are often sealed components. If yours are not, lightly grease them once every 1–2 years.

(2) The steering-head bearings should be greased on assembly (see p.60).

(3) If your swingarm and suspension linkage bearings have grease fittings, grease them regularly. Otherwise, dismantle the assembly once a year to clean and grease them (see p.87).

(4) Once or twice a year, you should lubricate control cables with silicone spray or light oil (see p.53).

(5) The speedometer drive gear and cable and the tachometer cable should all be greased once every 1–2 years.

(6) Lubricate switches with silicone spray regularly during the winter months.

(7) Telescopic forks are lubricated by their damping oil.

(8) The pivots and linkages of the control pedals and levers should be lightly greased about once a year.

(9) For lubrication details for the drive chain, see p.25.

(10) For engine oil details, see pp.42–43.

Plus (not shown on this bike):
Drive shaft See p.55.
Gearbox See p.44.
Two-stroke See p.18.

Oil and oil filter change

THE ENGINE IS CLEANED, cooled, and lubricated by oil. In a four-stroke engine, oil is pumped around the engine to moving parts, before returning to the sump, or reservoir. Gradually, the oil gets dirty and loses its viscosity, so it must be replaced regularly. There are two common lubrication systems used on four-stroke machines: on wet-sump bikes, oil is held in the engine's sump, while dry-sump bikes use a separate tank. A two-stroke engine burns oil during the combustion process, so it cannot be reused. Fresh oil – constantly being moved from oil tank to engine – never needs to be changed, but it must be filled up regularly. Many modern machines use a spin-on cartridge filter. This is housed in an integral metal case, which is screwed onto a thread mount on the engine. After the oil is drained from the engine, the filter can be removed.

OIL FILTERS

Oil filter

Filter cover   Oil seal

Spin-on filter

TYPICAL WET-SUMP OIL CHANGE

Socket

Container for
waste oil

1 DRAIN THE OIL

The drain plug is usually found under the engine. Take it out and drain the oil into a suitable container. Do this when the engine is hot so that the oil is more viscous, but beware of hot exhausts and hot oil. Dispose of old oil sensibly, preferably at an oil recycling center. On dry-sump engines, you must drain the tank and the engine.

2 REMOVE THE FILTER

Every time you change your oil, it's worth changing the oil filter. The filter type and access to it will vary between bikes. On this machine, it is located behind a cover at the front of the crankcase. Once the cover is removed, the filter can be withdrawn. When replacing the filter, make sure that all gaskets and seals, and the cover, are correctly seated.

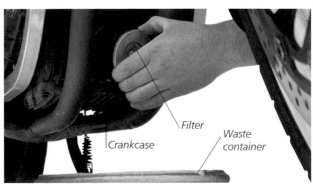

Filter

Crankcase

Waste
container

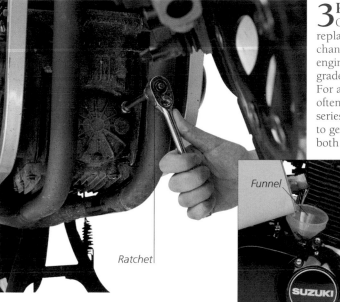

Ratchet

Funnel

3 REFILL THE ENGINE

Once you have securely replaced the drain plug and changed the filter, refill the engine with the recommended grade and quantity of oil. For a dry-sump engine, it is often necessary to perform a series of special procedures to get the correct level in both the engine and the oil tank. Typically, you should fill the tank before briefly running the engine. Fill up the tank, bleed the oil filter, and recheck the level – see your shop manual for specific details.

SPIN-ON FILTER OIL CHANGE

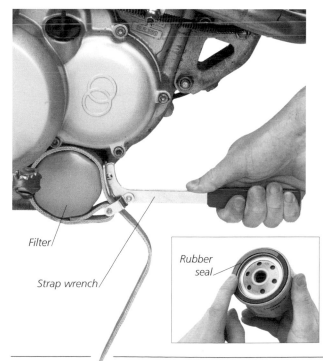

Filter

Strap wrench

Rubber seal

1 REMOVE THE FILTER

A spin-on filter has a metal case and screws onto a thread mount on the engine. Use a strap wrench to remove the old filter. The strap wraps tightly around the filter, gripping it as it is turned, thus giving you a lot of leverage.

2 FIT THE NEW FILTER

Before screwing on the new filter, it is a good idea to smear some oil around its rubber seal. This will help to create an oil-tight seal. When screwing it on, turn the filter onto the mount by hand until it is tight, then use the strap wrench to make sure it is fully secured. However, be careful not to overtighten it.

Gearbox oil

ALL TWO-STROKE BIKES – and some four-strokes – have gearbox lubrication systems separate from those of the engines. Because the two functions are separate, you can use more specialized oils, which will have longer service lives. Gearbox oil should be changed according to the manufacturer's recommendations; every 10,000–12,000 miles (16,000–19,000 kilometers) or once a year is typical.

GEARBOX OIL CHANGE

1 DRAIN THE OLD OIL
Unless it leaks or there is a problem, the gearbox's oil level should remain constant. On some machines, a screw is provided for checking (right). If oil emerges when the screw is removed, there is sufficient oil in the gearbox. A drain plug is located under the engine casing; unscrew this to drain the oil. Check your owner's manual to make sure you are removing the correct bolt. Drain the old oil into a container for disposal. As with all oil, it will drain more easily if it is warm. If necessary, replace the plug's gasket or sealing washer. Clean the drain plug and put it back. Tighten it before refilling the gearbox.

Gear
lever

Level-check
screw

2 REPLACE THE OIL
Refill the gearbox with the quantity and grade of oil specified by the manufacturer. The filler hole may be awkward to access, so use a funnel to prevent spills. Replace the cap.

GEARBOX LUBRICATION
Most modern four-strokes have a combined engine/gearbox lubrication system with a pump to circulate the oil; this eases oil changes. All two-strokes (in which the crankcases are used in the fuel/air mix induction) and some four-strokes have a self-contained gearbox/primary-drive lubrication system. Normally, this is a simple sump in which the gears run; their motion throws the oil around to lubricate the bearings. If the bike is used for short trips in winter, gearbox condensation can occur. More frequent oil changes will reduce the problem.

Air filter

THE AIR FILTER prevents dust and dirt from getting
sucked into the engine where they can cause harm.
A clogged air filter, however, will impair the bike's
performance. The air filter is housed in the "air
box," usually found under the fuel tank or the seat.
For machine-specific information on access, and
recommended inspection intervals, see your
owner's manual or shop manual. Modern machines
tend to use paper or oil-impregnated foam filters.

Paper filter

REPLACING THE FILTER

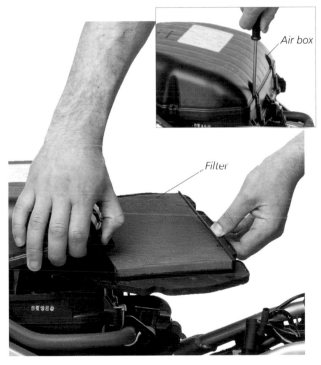

Air box

Filter

1 OPEN THE AIR BOX
Typically, the air box is a
plastic container in two parts,
held together with screws.
Undo the screws and lift the
top part of the air box. The
filter can now be withdrawn.

2 REMOVE THE OLD FILTER
When removing the filter
from its housing, note which
way it fits. Gently tap the
filter, intake side downward,
on a hard surface to dislodge
dirt particles. Use a soft brush
to aid this process. Ideally,
you should use compressed
air to blow dirt back through
the filter. These procedures
will enhance the life of the
filter. After you have cleaned
it, you should inspect the
filter for damage. If it is torn
or is particularly dirty, it
should be replaced.

OIL-IMPREGNATED FOAM FILTERS
This type of filter should be cleaned by
soaking in a nonflammable cleaning solvent,
then gently squeezing it to remove the dirt
and solvent. Next, immerse it in fresh oil and
squeeze again to remove any excess oil.

Fuel system checkup and clean

CARBURETORS CONTROL THE MIXTURE of fuel and air entering the engine, and are very sensitive to poor conditions. Dirt and water in the fuel supply can cause erratic engine running or stop the bike altogether. Drain the tank completely about once a year to remove unwanted water and dirt. Inspect and clean fuel filters and carburetor float bowls at the same time. Fuel lines and sealing washers should be checked for leaks or cracking; replace them every few years. If the bike has been standing for more than a few weeks, the fuel will go bad, so replace it. Additives in fuel can leave a brown coating on carburetors that can impede fuel flow. This coating should be removed with paint thinner and a soft brush or cloth.

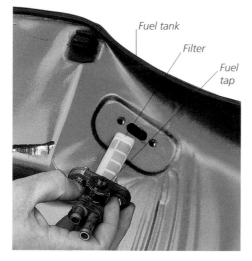

Fuel tank

Filter

Fuel tap

CHECKING AND CLEANING

1 DRAIN THE TANK
Remove the tank (see pp.32–33), and drain the fuel from it. Remove the fuel tap(s) and flush the tank. To do this, put some fresh fuel in the tank, block the tap holes with a cloth and your finger, and shake the fuel around. Drain the tank again.

2 INSPECT AND CLEAN THE FILTERS
The fuel tap has a filter protruding into the tank. Check it periodically (while the tank is empty) and clean it with fresh fuel on a soft brush or cloth before blowing compressed air through it in the reverse direction to fuel flow. Some bikes have a second filter where the fuel line connects to the carburetor body.

3 DRAIN AND INSPECT THE FLOAT BOWL
Any dirt or water that gets past the filters will arrive at the carburetor's fuel reservoir, the float bowl. It is from here that the fuel is drawn through the carburetor jets; these are calibrated passages normally in the form of a brass screw. The float bowl is attached to the bottom of the carburetor by screw(s) or clip. Most float bowls have a drain screw so that you can drain the fuel before removing the bowl. Clean the float bowl with fuel on a soft cloth or brush, and remove varnish deposits with carburetor cleaner or paint thinner and a soft brush.

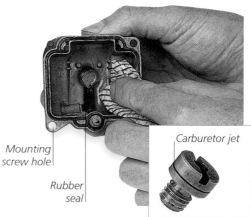

Mounting screw hole

Rubber seal

Carburetor jet

Spark plugs

THE IGNITION SYSTEM'S final component is the spark plug, which puts a spark in the cylinder at the critical moment – more than 100 every second, in temperatures of up to 4,500°F (2,500°C). Not surprisingly, it needs occasional inspection, adjustment, and replacement. When replacing, use the correct specification. Different manufacturers use different identification codes, but all major companies should have a plug of the correct specification.

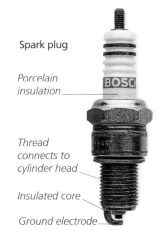

Spark plug

Porcelain insulation

Thread connects to cylinder head

Insulated core

Ground electrode

REMOVING AND CHECKING

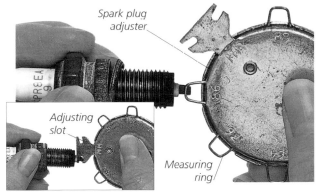

1 REMOVE THE PLUG
Motorcycle spark plugs come in three common thread sizes – 20.6mm, 18mm, and 16mm. For removal, use either a box wrench of the correct size or a ratchet and plug socket. When removing the plug, make sure that no dirt falls into the cylinder.

Spark plug adjuster

Adjusting slot

Measuring ring

2 CHECK CONDITION
The plug's core should be brown, tan, or gray in color, and there should be no soot or white deposits. Electrodes should be in good condition and the gap between them as specified in your shop manual. You can check that the gap is correct by using either the measuring rings on your spark plug adjuster or a feeler gauge.

3 ADJUST THE GAP
Reset the spark plug gap by bending the ground electrode with the appropriate slot on your spark plug adjuster. Replace the spark plug and tighten it to a snug fit by hand. To secure it fully, tighten it with your wrench or ratchet.

COPPER GREASING
A modern engine's spark plug rarely needs removing, but when it does, it may be very tight. To ease the next removal, sparingly apply copper grease to the thread before replacing it.

Brakes explained

BRAKES WORK BY using friction to slow a rotating disc or drum – the rotor – turning kinetic energy into heat. Metal-backed fiber pads or shoes are pressed onto the rotor by a hydraulic or mechanical system to create the friction. During this process, the pads or shoes are subject to wear. If they are replaced within their specified service limits, wear on the rotor should be minimal, unless the machine has traveled many miles or received severe use. Regular inspection and replacement of the pads or shoes are essential to keep the brakes in good condition. Many pads and shoes contain asbestos, so wear a dust mask and be careful while working on brakes. Always refer to the shop manual for machine-specific information.

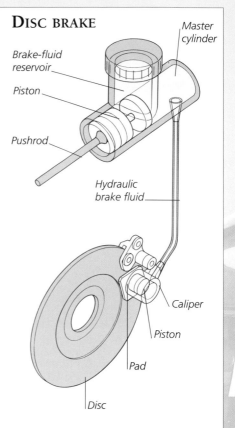

DISC BRAKE

Master cylinder

Brake-fluid reservoir

Piston

Pushrod

Hydraulic brake fluid

Caliper

Piston

Pad

Disc

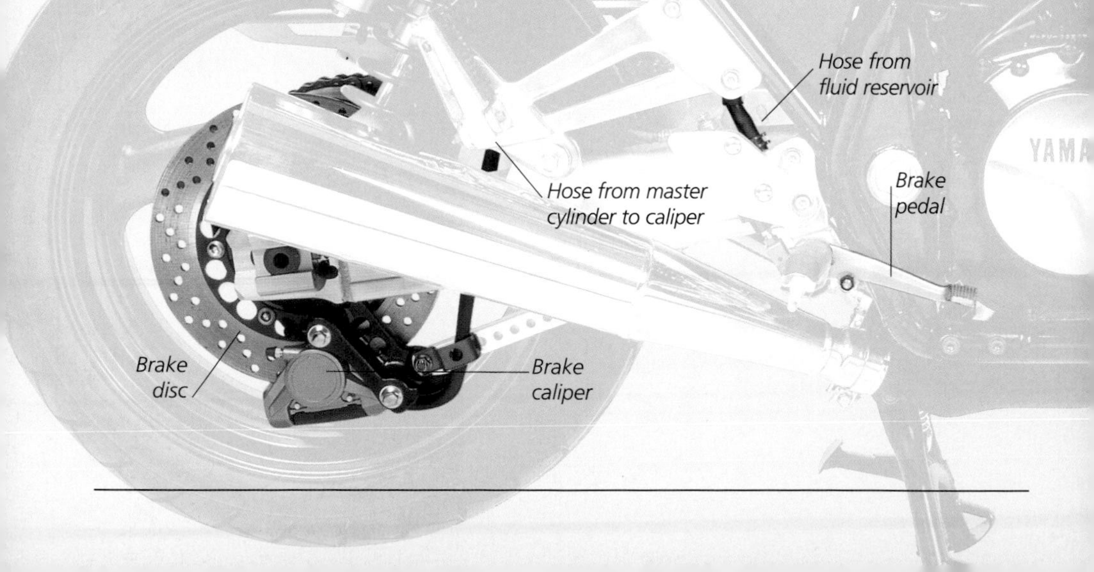

Hose from fluid reservoir

Hose from master cylinder to caliper

Brake pedal

Brake disc

Brake caliper

YAMA

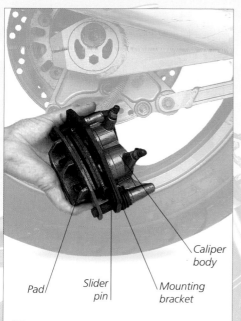

DRUM BRAKE

Air-cooling scoop

Speedometer drive cavity

Operating arm

Torque arm

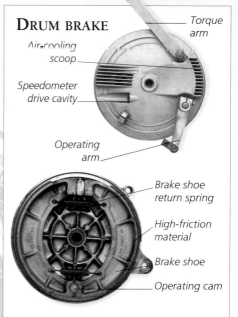

Brake shoe return spring

High-friction material

Brake shoe

Operating cam

Caliper body

Pad

Slider pin

Mounting bracket

FLOATING-CALIPER DISC BRAKE

CALIPER DESIGNS

To slow a disc, equal force must be used on both sides. There are two main caliper types. Piston calipers are rigidly mounted and have pistons in matched pairs on each side of the disc. "Floating" or sliding calipers have pistons on just one side. As the brake is applied, the caliper slides on pins, pulling the pads on the other side into contact with the disc.

DRUM BRAKES

The shoes and operating cams of drum brakes are hidden inside the drum, and a mechanical, rather than hydraulic, operating system is used. This means that corrosion is not such a big problem as on disc brakes, and that the operating system must be adjusted regularly.

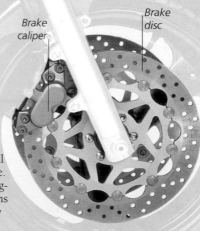

Brake caliper

Brake disc

DISC-BRAKE PAD

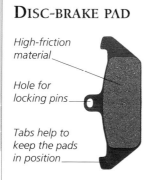

High-friction material

Hole for locking pins

Tabs help to keep the pads in position

RETAINING PINS

Brake pads are usually retained in position by pins. In floating calipers, the same pins may allow the caliper to slide in relationship to the mounting bracket. Corrosion on the pins will impair brake performance. When you change floating-caliper pads, clean the pins and lubricate them lightly with copper grease.

Brakes check and change

THE BRAKES SHOULD BE INSPECTED regularly and the pads or shoes replaced when necessary. Early replacement will prolong the life of other components and keep the brakes working more efficiently. Consult your shop manual for the exact procedure and the critical wear limits for your bike. Remember that brake fluid is corrosive, brake dust is toxic, and you should never pull the brake lever while the pads are removed or the caliper is off the disc. Also, be careful not to contaminate the friction material with oil or dirt. The performance of the brakes is critical to your bike's safety, so, after fitting new pads or doing any brake-related work, apply the brake several times to restore "feel" to the system, and use the brakes gently until they have been broken in.

CHANGING DISC BRAKE PADS

CHECK PAD WEAR

The procedure for checking and changing the pads varies between the types of caliper. Piston calipers often have a cover, which can be pried off with a screwdriver, in the top of the caliper body to allow the pads to be easily checked. Floating calipers may have to be removed to allow the pads to be checked and changed. The following procedure is for a typical piston caliper setup.

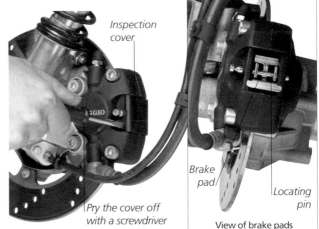

Inspection cover

Pry the cover off with a screwdriver

Brake pad

Locating pin

View of brake pads

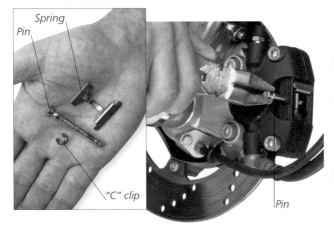

Spring

Pin

"C" clip

Pin

1 REMOVE CALIPER PIN AND SPRING

Disc brake pads are retained by pins that pass through the caliper body. The pins are, in turn, usually retained by either an "R" clip, a "C" clip, or a split pin. Split pins should not be reused. When removing any of these clips or pins, be careful not to lose anything, because they are *not* supplied with new pads. Replacement can be aided by making notes on the order of removal.

2 CHANGE THE PADS

Using pliers, take the pads out. They will be thinner than the new ones due to wear. To make the new pads fit, you may have to ease the piston back into the caliper – this should not require much force. Don't pull the brake lever while the pads are out.

3 CHECK THE SEALS

Check the piston's dust seals for any splits. Reassemble the unit in reverse order.

Withdraw the pads with pliers

Seal

Piston

DRUM BRAKE SHOE CHECKING AND CHANGING

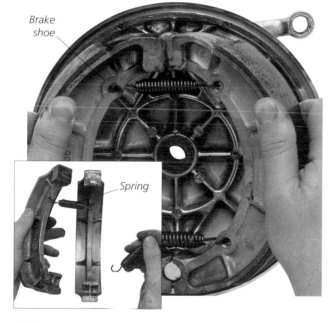

Brake shoe

Spring

CHECK SHOE WEAR

The internal components of drum brakes cannot be inspected without removing the wheel from the bike (see pp.26–27). Having removed the wheel, you may then pull the back plate from the brake drum to inspect the shoes. For information regarding shoe-wear limits you should consult your manual.

1 REMOVE THE SHOES

The drum brake shoes are retained in position by strong springs (some bikes may also have clips on the pivots). To remove the shoes, fold them together to relax the tension on the springs. Be careful not to catch your fingers.

2 LUBRICATE AND REPLACE

Replacement is a reversal of the removal process. Again, be careful not to get your fingers caught. Before replacing the shoes, it is worth putting a light smear of grease on the operating cam. Before reassembling the wheel, remove dust from the drum using a soft brush. Be careful not to inhale the asbestos dust, and remember to dispose of it carefully.

Hydraulic fluid

TO DISCOVER LEAKS AT AN early stage, hydraulic operating systems need to be given regular visual checkups. Leaks allow fluid to escape from the system and allow air to enter it. Hydraulic fluid absorbs water from the atmosphere, and this causes the brakes to act less efficiently; the braking performance is reduced and a spongy feeling is given to the brake lever. Air must be removed by bleeding the system, for which you will need an assistant. The fluid should be changed every two to three years.

BLEEDING HYDRAULIC FLUID

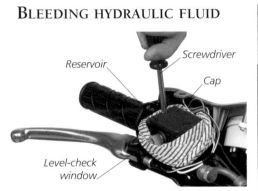

Reservoir   Screwdriver   Cap   Level-check window

1 REMOVE THE RESERVOIR CAP
Check the fluid level via a translucent fluid reservoir or a level-checking window. Remove the cap, which in this example is secured by screws. Underneath the cap is a diaphragm. Lift this clear to expose the fluid.

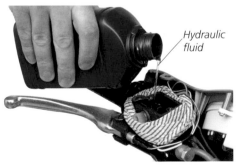

Hydraulic fluid

2 FILL UP THE FLUID
Always use hydraulic fluid from a new, unopened container, and be sure it is compatible with the fluid already in the system. Fill up the fluid and replace the diaphragm and cap. Do not spill any fluid – it is corrosive.

Bleed nipple   Brake caliper

Hydraulic fluid   Plastic tube   Hydraulic hose

3 BLEED THE BRAKES
Brake calipers have at least one bleed nipple. Fit a clear plastic tube to the nipple and put the other end in a little hydraulic fluid in a jar. Loosen the nipple one turn and squeeze the brake lever gently; fluid will flow from the caliper. Tighten the nipple, and release the lever. If the fluid in the tube contains bubbles, repeat until it is clear. Fill up the reservoir during bleeding, but pull the brake only when the diaphragm is fitted. Repeat for each caliper.

Cable lubrication

ALTHOUGH HYDRAULIC OPERATING SYSTEMS are common for disc brakes, most other controls use cables. The cable's condition will affect the "feel" of the mechanism, so for the precise operation that throttles, clutches, and brakes require, cables must be correctly adjusted, routed, and lubricated. While oiling, inspect the inner cable for signs of fraying. For throttle cables, you usually dismantle the throttle assembly, while for lubrication, you must disconnect the cable. On handlebar levers, the screw adjuster must be screwed in after the locknut is released.

1 REMOVE THE CABLE
Line up the slots in the adjuster and the lever and fully loosen the cable. Pull the cable outer away from the lever to clear the adjuster, then away from the bike so the inner cable comes through the slot. If you can't get the cable outer clear of the adjuster, pull the lever and release it slowly while pulling the outer away.

2 LUBRICATE
The nipple at the end of the cable should come out of its housing very easily, thus leaving the cable end free. Lubricate the cable. The easiest way to do this is with a cable-lubricating tool placed over the cable's free end. Put the cable inner into the slot in the tool, and secure it into place by tightening the screw on the side. Use a can of spray lubricant to oil the cable via the small holes in the tool.

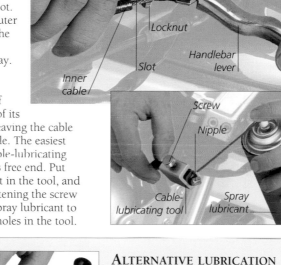

Screw adjuster

Slot

Locknut

Handlebar lever

Slot

Inner cable

Screw

Nipple

Cable-lubricating tool

Spray lubricant

Greaseproof paper funnel

ALTERNATIVE LUBRICATION
An alternative cable lubrication method involves making a funnel using greaseproof paper and tape. Tape the funnel to the cable outer, near its end, and pour a small amount of oil into the funnel. The oil flow can be assisted by moving the cable inner; this is done by pulling on the nipple. You may find that to do a thorough lubrication job, the best course of action is to disconnect the cable completely at both ends.

Transmission explained

THE TRANSMISSION SYSTEM USUALLY consists of a clutch, a gearbox, and a chain final drive, and conveys power from the engine to the rear wheel. The gearbox allows the engine to be used effectively, without stalling or over-revving and, unless abused, it should be reliable. If the gear change becomes notchy or clunky, the condition of the clutch and the operating linkage should be checked first. The clutch acts as a mechanical switch, completing or breaking the connection between engine and gearbox when the rider changes gear or stops (see pp.82–83). The final-drive chain transfers power from the gearbox to the rear wheel, although some bikes use shaft or belt drive (see right). On many scooters and mopeds, the transmission is designed to provide an automatic variable ratio and clutch system that needs minimal maintenance.

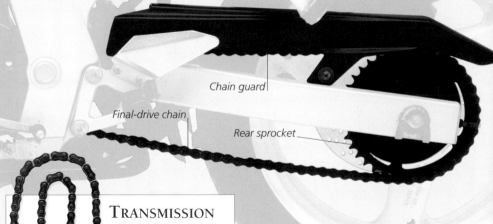

Chain guard

Final-drive chain

Rear sprocket

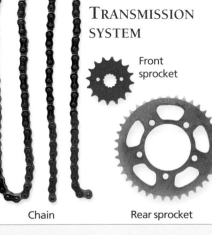

TRANSMISSION SYSTEM

Front sprocket

Chain

Rear sprocket

DRIVE CHAINS

There are two types of chain in common use: conventional and O-ring chains. Most modern high-performance bikes use O-ring chains, which have lubricant in the rollers kept in place by O rings. Chains are joined using a special link, which may be one of two types. A split link uses a spring clip to join the link, while a soft link is fitted using a special tool. Usually, chain size is specified as a three-figure number, but when buying a chain you need to specify the number of links. If necessary, a chain can be shortened using a link breaker.

THE CUSH DRIVE

It is important that the transmission include a shock absorber or cush drive to smooth the power delivery to the rear wheel. On chain drive bikes, this is usually a rubber spacer in the rear hub between the sprocket and the wheel. If the rubber is compressed or damaged, slack will appear in the system. The cush drive condition should be checked regularly and, if necessary, the rubbers should be replaced.

Cush-drive rubber

Sprocket carrier

OTHER DRIVE SYSTEMS

Side view

Top view

TOOTHED-BELT DRIVE

Some motorcycles, including modern Harley-Davidsons and some lightweight Kawasakis, have a toothed belt instead of a final-drive chain. The belt is quiet and requires little maintenance, but replacement may involve removing the entire swingarm assembly (see p.87) to fit the endless belt to the gearbox output pulley. Check the pulley's condition since stones can damage it and reduce the belt's life.

CONSTANTLY VARIABLE TRANSMISSION

Many lightweight scooters and mopeds use a form of "automatic" gearbox based on the use of centrifugal clutches and V-belt systems. The straightforward task of replacing V-belts must be undertaken at manufacturer-specified intervals. In the case of the bike shown here, the front pulley is split by removing the center bolt. This facilitates the removal of the belt from the pulleys.

SHAFT DRIVE

The most maintenance-free final-drive system is shaft drive. Maintenance is limited to changing the oil in the bevel gear housing at specified intervals. A drain plug is located at the bottom of the casing and a filler at the top. Refill with the correct grade and quantity of lubricant. Refer to your owner's manual for machine-specific details.

Drain plug

Filler hole

Chain and sprocket replacement

A DRIVE CHAIN'S LIFE expectancy depends on its quality, the bike's power, and, crucially, chain maintenance. A worn chain is inefficient and dangerous, and should be replaced when it has "stretched" as little as two percent more than its original length. The sprockets on which the chain runs may outlast one chain, and early replacement of worn chains will prolong sprocket life. If the new chain is to be connected with a split link, replacement is straightforward. Chains joined with a soft link are more difficult: a special tool is needed for the fitting process and it may be easier to entrust the job to a mechanic. The chain is probably the dirtiest component on the bike so clean the area first. See your shop manual for machine-specific details.

THE SPLIT LINK

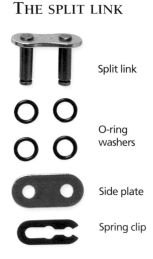

Split link

O-ring washers

Side plate

Spring clip

REMOVAL AND REPLACEMENT PROCEDURES

Clutch cable

1 CHECK CHAIN WEAR

Try pulling the chain away from the rear of the sprocket. If it lifts enough to let you see between the teeth of the sprocket, it means it is badly worn. Check the sprocket teeth for signs of wear. Also check to see if you have used up all of the adjustment on the axle.

2 ACCESS THE SPROCKETS

To access the sprockets, the rear wheel must be clear of the ground: if your bike has no center stand, use a bike stand. The front sprocket has a guard, which may include part of the clutch-operating mechanism, that must be removed to access the sprocket. It may also help to remove the chain guard.

3 REMOVE THE CHAIN

If a split link is fitted, it is easily removed. Using pliers, squeeze the spring clip off the pins, remove the side plate, and push the split link through. Having removed the split link, you can now pull the chain clear of the sprockets. On bikes with a soft link, you will have to use a special tool, or (very carefully) a grinder followed by a punch, to remove a link.

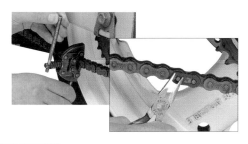

4 LOOSEN THE SPROCKETS

It is often easier to loosen the retaining bolts on the sprockets while the chain is still on and the wheels are still attached to the bike. Get someone to operate the brake lever while you undo the nuts.

5 CHANGE THE FRONT SPROCKET

Remove the bolts from the front sprocket, and slide it off its shaft. The new sprocket can now be fitted.

6 PUT ON THE NEW CHAIN

The new chain will be shorter than the old one, so it is important that the rear wheel is moved forward. Loosen the axle adjustment bolts accordingly, making sure you turn each bolt by the same amount so as not to misalign the wheels. Put newspaper under the working area to prevent the chain from getting dirty if it falls to the floor. Feed the chain onto the rear sprocket, then along the top of the swingarm and down onto the front sprocket. This will allow you to fit the linkage components on the lower run of the chain, which is more accessible.

7 ADJUST THE TENSION

Fit the split link with the spring clip's closed end facing the direction of chain travel. Make sure that the chain is joined and adjusted correctly, and all bolts are tight. Finally, check wheel alignment (see pp.58–59). A soft link, recommended on high-power bikes, can only be fitted using an expensive tool. If necessary, use a split link and take the bike to a mechanic.

Wheel alignment

IN ORDER FOR A BIKE to handle well, its wheels must be in line. Even on new machines, the wheels are often misaligned, and when the rear wheel is moved to adjust the chain, the wheel alignment can be upset further. To check the alignment you can use one, or preferably two, straight edges, which must be longer than the bike. If these are unavailable, it is possible to use string, but this is a less accurate and more complicated method.

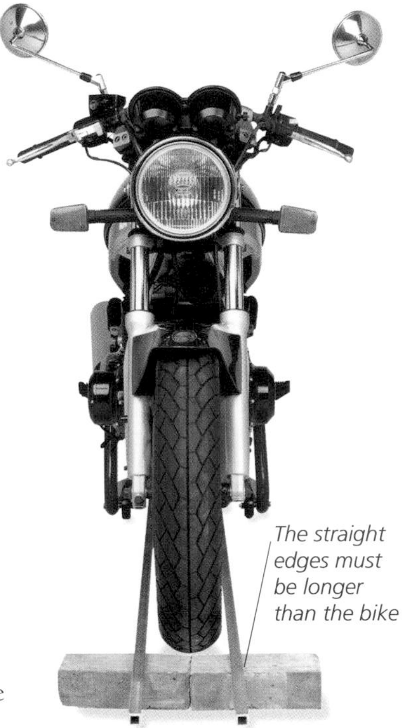

ALIGNING THE WHEELS

1 SET THE STRAIGHT EDGES
Secure the bike in an upright position, preferably using a bike stand. Place two bricks or blocks of wood of equal height at both the bike's front and rear, and run one straight edge down each side of the machine. They should be positioned as high as possible and not touch any part of the bike except the front and rear edges of the rear tire. Set the steering straight ahead. The front wheel, which is thinner than the rear one, should be parallel to the straight edges and have an equal gap on each side of it.

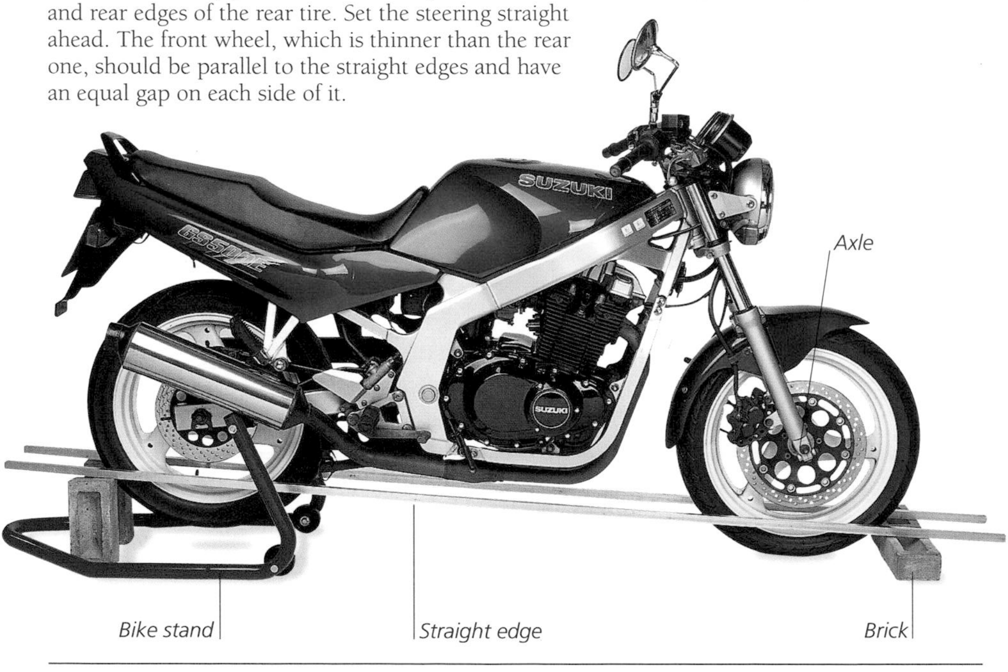

The straight edges must be longer than the bike

Axle

Bike stand

Straight edge

Brick

2 MEASURE THE OFFSET

Measure the distance of both the front and rear edges of the front tire from the straight edge. This figure is the "offset," and should be equal to half the difference in width of the two tires. To carry out this procedure using string (inset), put the bike in gear and loop the string around the back of the rear wheel. Run the string down to the front wheel. Pull it so it touches the front and rear edges of the rear tire, and measure the offset between the string and the front and rear edges of the front tire.

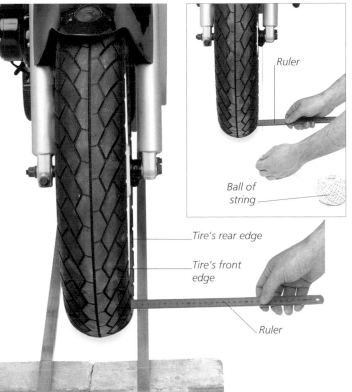

Ruler

Ball of string

Tire's rear edge

Tire's front edge

Ruler

Axle adjustment nuts

3 ADJUST THE AXLE

To alter the alignment, you must move the rear axle on one side. Loosen the axle nut and, to preserve the correct chain tension, turn the adjuster bolt on the opposite side to the chain in small increments. Make sure that the axle remains in contact with the adjuster. Retighten the axle and recheck the alignment. Repeat this procedure until the alignment is set. If you cannot set the alignment correctly, the bike's frame may be bent.

Steering and suspension

To MAINTAIN THE HANDLING OF your motorcycle, the chassis must be in optimum condition. Its ability to perform correctly can be badly affected by worn bearings. Before attempting to rectify this, make sure that any detected free play is not the result of a loose bolt or fastener.

WORN STEERING-HEAD BEARINGS CHECK

Support the bike – making sure that it is stable and secure – with its front wheel off the ground. Loosen or remove any steering damper fitted. Turn the handlebars from side to side – any roughness or notches that are felt are evidence of worn bearings. Replacement is the only cure. This means the complete disassembly of the front of the bike, a job beyond the scope of this book.

LOOSE STEERING-HEAD BEARINGS CHECK

With the front wheel off the ground and after making sure the bike is securely supported, grasp the front wheel and try to move it both backward and forward. If there is any evidence of movement, it is an indication that the headraces are loose.

SWINGARM BEARINGS CHECK

With the rear wheel off the ground, grasp it firmly and push it from side to side. Make sure that any movement detected is not caused by the bike moving or from loose wheel bearings (see "Wheel bearing checks" opposite). Place your other hand between the swingarm and the frame to try to detect movement. If any play is detected, the bearings must be replaced. (some motorcycles use taper roller bearings, which can be adjusted.) When you come to replacing the swingarm bearings, you should consult a shop manual specific to your machine.

WHEEL BEARINGS CHECK

Lift the wheel off the ground and turn it to detect roughness. Try rocking the wheel from side to side at its top. If you detect movement, rotate the wheel and try at another spot. If roughness and movement are present, you should replace the bearings. For details of how to do so, you should consult your shop manual.

SUSPENSION LINKAGE CHECK

Modern rear suspension systems often use a single suspension unit operated from the swingarm via a linkage. The linkage bearings operate under extreme loads and are often poorly lubricated. Worn bearings result in play in the system, which can mean impaired rear suspension operation. Check for play by using a piece of wood to gently lift the rear wheel upward while feeling for play in the linkage with your other hand.

ADJUSTING THE STEERING-HEAD BEARINGS

1 LOOSEN THE TOP YOKE

Make sure the bike is well supported with the front wheel off the ground. Remove the front wheel – this lightens the forks and eases the job. The bearings are located at the top and bottom of the frame tube through which the steering stem passes. Loosen the top yoke nut, the fork-leg clamps on the yoke, and the slim castellated nut(s) above the upper bearing. The arrangement of nuts and bolts will vary between machines – for example, there is no top yoke on a scooter – so consult your shop manual.

2 RETIGHTEN THE BEARINGS

Support the steering head with one hand under the bottom yoke, and tighten the castellated nut with your other hand. Turn the steering so you can feel as the bearings get tighter – hand-tight on the nut should be enough. The forks should move without feeling tight or notchy, but without any slack. When you are satisfied with the setting, tighten the locknut without moving the correctly set nut below it. Finally, retighten the stem top nut and any other fasteners disturbed in the process.

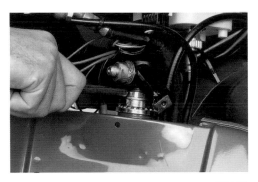

More complex tasks

THE AREAS THAT ARE COVERED in this section are complicated, time-consuming, or both. They may well require special service tools or replacement parts. If you get the jobs wrong, you will make your bike worse than it was before. However, doing the tasks correctly will restore your bike to top condition, save you money, and make you feel good. You will need the correct shop manual for your machine to handle work in these areas. The following section is an introduction that will help you understand what you have to do and why you have to do it. Cleanliness, preparation, and patience are essential. Also, you must make sure that you have close at hand all the tools and parts necessary to complete the job. At all times, you should be vigilant about dirt: it must not be allowed to enter the engine or other delicate components. If you happen to get stuck while working on your bike, stop, put down your tools, and think about the problem before you go on. It is amazing how often this helps.

SPECIAL TOOLS

The jobs in this section require greater expertise and accuracy than those in earlier sections. Special tools are needed to measure accurately gaps, torque, or timing. Other special tools may be necessary to remove or replace particular components. Most of these tools are expensive, which eliminates possible DIY savings. Buy them only if you really must – borrowing is cheaper – and use and store them with care.

Timing gun
Modern electronic ignition rarely needs attention, but if it does, and if you decide to tackle it, you will need a timing gun.

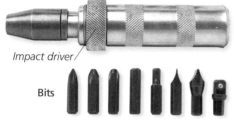

Impact driver

Bits

Impact driver
This tool is useful for removing stubborn fasteners, providing a combination of shock and torque. Use it carefully to avoid damaging the fastener.

Oil seal tool
To fit oil seals to inverted forks, a special tool is necessary. Despite its simplicity, it is very expensive. If you can't borrow one, take the job to a specialist.

Tool for external measuring

Small spanner wrench

Special spanner wrench
Each bike has some fasteners to which access is awkward or the size is unusual. It may be necessary to get a certain shape or size of wrench to suit a particular job.

Torque wrench
This tool measures the force that is being exerted on the fastener you are tightening.

Tool for internal measuring

Flats for wrench

Feeler gauge

Vernier gauge
This is a useful tool for measuring small items, but it is rarely essential.

Feeler gauges
If you are likely to be checking valve clearances or adjusting contact breakers, you will need a set of these (cheap) tools.

Special pullers
The proper factory tools are best for flywheel removal. Make sure you use them correctly.

Vacuum gauges
If you are a committed DIY mechanic, it may be worth investing in a set of vacuum gauges – or a manometer – to balance carburetors.

Four-strokes explained

THE INTERNAL COMBUSTION ENGINE operates by creating a controlled "explosion" within a sealed cylinder. The expansion of gases caused by the explosion forces a piston – which forms the base of the cylinder – downward. This linear movement is converted into rotational movement by a crankshaft connected via a rod to the piston. In the four-stroke engine, the admission and exhaust of the gases from the cylinder are controlled by valves in the cylinder head operated by a camshaft.

THE FOUR-STROKE SEQUENCE

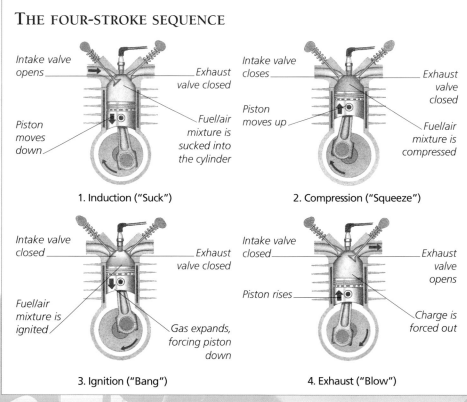

Intake valve opens

Exhaust valve closed

Piston moves down

Fuel/air mixture is sucked into the cylinder

1. Induction ("Suck")

Intake valve closes

Exhaust valve closed

Piston moves up

Fuel/air mixture is compressed

2. Compression ("Squeeze")

Intake valve closed

Exhaust valve closed

Fuel/air mixture is ignited

Gas expands, forcing piston down

3. Ignition ("Bang")

Intake valve closed

Exhaust valve opens

Piston rises

Charge is forced out

4. Exhaust ("Blow")

TIMING

The precise moment at which valves open and close and the fuel mix is ignited is critical to the operation of the engine. The sequence, as shown above, seems logical, but it isn't that simple. The valves remain open for longer than the 180° period suggested in the diagram to obtain maximum efficiency from the engine. The speed at which the engine runs – at 6,000rpm, the piston stops and starts 100 times a second, and each valve opens and closes 50 times a second – means that gases flowing into and out of the engine move very fast and at very high pressure.

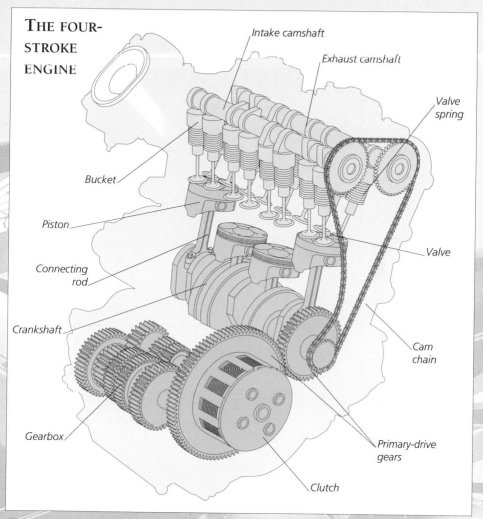

THE FOUR-STROKE ENGINE

Intake camshaft

Exhaust camshaft

Valve spring

Bucket

Piston

Connecting rod

Crankshaft

Valve

Cam chain

Gearbox

Primary-drive gears

Clutch

FOUR-STROKE COMPONENTS

The components of the four-stroke internal combustion engine are divisible into two areas, which must work in synchronization: those concerned with converting the expansion of the gas into rotational movement (piston, cylinder, connecting rod, and crankshaft), and those that relate to the admission and exhaust of gases from the cylinder (valves, cylinder head, and camshaft). Most modern engines have their camshaft (or camshafts) mounted above the cylinder head and are usually driven by a chain running from the crankshaft. Older designs have the camshaft mounted closer to the crank and use pushrods to transfer the lifting force to the cylinder head. Cam lobes control the valve openings. The engine's metal components expand when hot, so there must be some slack in the valve-train system. The amount of slack is critical to its effective operation, and it will alter as the engine wears. To create the slack, a specified gap is set in the valve train between the valve and the camshaft. Apart from oil changes, the checking and resetting of the gap is the most fundamental four-stroke maintenance task.

FOUR-STROKES EXPLAINED continued

THE CAMSHAFT

Engine "breathing" is controlled by camshafts. When the valves open and close, and how wide they open, greatly affects the engine's performance. Many modern bikes have two camshafts: one for the intake valves and one for the exhaust.

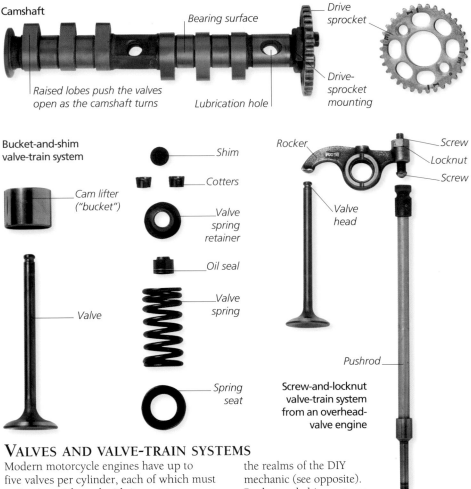

Camshaft

Bearing surface

Drive sprocket

Raised lobes push the valves open as the camshaft turns

Lubrication hole

Drive-sprocket mounting

Bucket-and-shim valve-train system

Shim

Cotters

Cam lifter ("bucket")

Valve spring retainer

Oil seal

Valve spring

Valve

Spring seat

Rocker

Screw

Locknut

Screw

Valve head

Pushrod

Screw-and-locknut valve-train system from an overhead-valve engine

VALVES AND VALVE-TRAIN SYSTEMS

Modern motorcycle engines have up to five valves per cylinder, each of which must maintain a tight seal with its seat to prevent engine inefficiency and loss of compression. The valves are kept closed by springs and run within guides, which are firmly positioned in the cylinder heads. With time and use, valve guides and stems are prone to wear.

Two types of valve-train systems are common in motorcycles. Screw-and-locknut systems are simple to check and adjust, and are within the realms of the DIY mechanic (see opposite). Bucket-and-shim systems may be a better engineering solution, but they are much more complicated to adjust. This job can involve special tools or the removal of the camshafts. For a DIY mechanic, it is a time-consuming and complex job, and one that most owners would be better advised to entrust to a professional mechanic (see p.68).

Four-stroke maintenance

VALVE CLEARANCES ARE CHECKED with the engine cold and the cylinder on which you are working set at tdc on the compression stroke so that both valves are fully closed. Markers on the flywheel and the camshaft sprockets must be aligned to ensure that the engine is in the correct position. On each cylinder, the tdc/compression position is different. Removing the spark plugs allows the engine to be turned to the correct point using a socket or spanner wrench on the crankshaft end nut. Details of access, the correct gap, and timing marks are provided in your shop manual.

SCREW-AND-LOCKNUT ADJUSTMENT

1 CHECK THE VALVE CLEARANCE

With the engine set at tdc on the compression stroke, slide a feeler gauge of the specified thickness between the head of the valve and the rocker. It should fit snugly, with some resistance felt. If it feels loose or it won't fit, the clearance must be adjusted.

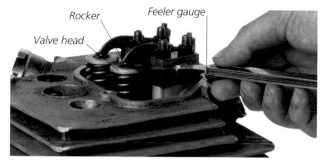

Rocker

Feeler gauge

Valve head

Screw

2 ADJUST THE VALVE CLEARANCE

With the feeler gauge still between the rocker and the valve head, loosen the locknut on the adjuster and tighten the screw to finger-tightness. Make sure that the screw doesn't move while retightening the locknut. Finally, recheck the clearance.

PROBLEMS

The four-stroke engine, despite its complexity, is reliable provided that it is correctly lubricated and cooled. However, camshaft drive chains wear and their tensioners can be unreliable; both of these things become apparent when a rattle develops. The chain is usually endless, and much of the engine must be dismantled to remove or replace it. This complex job is beyond the scope of this book. Some engines have a belt-driven camshaft, the replacement of which is a regular service job (see p.69).

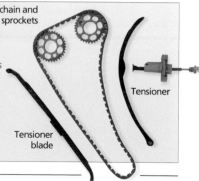

Cam chain and sprockets

Tensioner

Tensioner blade

BUCKET-AND-SHIM ADJUSTMENT

1 CHECK THE CLEARANCE

Slide the feeler gauge into position between the camshaft and the "bucket." It must fit, but a little resistance should be felt. Because resetting the gap correctly requires the replacement of the shim, you need to know by how much the gap is too large or too small. Use feeler gauges to assess the size of the gap. This process must be repeated on every valve. Keep notes, because the actual size of the gap must be deducted from the correct gap size to find out how much thicker or thinner the new shim needs to be. You must remove the old shim to assess the size you need.

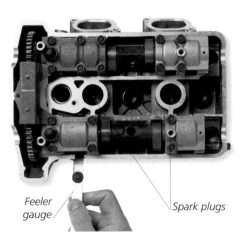

Feeler gauge

Spark plugs

2 REMOVE AND REPLACE THE SHIMS

Having established that the shims need changing, it may be worth having it done professionally. However, if you decide to do it yourself, make sure that you have the proper shop manuals and a decent working environment. In the example shown here, the shim is located beneath the bucket. Once the camshafts have been removed, the bucket can be lifted off the valve to reveal the shim. This can easily be achieved by using a small magnet, which you can also use to remove the shim.

The thickness of the shim is indicated by a number that is etched onto its surface (see below).

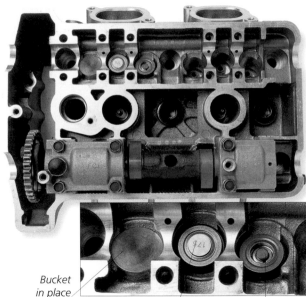

Bucket in place

Remove the bucket to reveal the shim

Remove the shim to reveal the top of the valve

Different thickness shims

MULTICYLINDER BIKES

You should allow yourself most of a day the first time you attempt this complicated task on a multicylinder bike. Make accurate notes as you work to make sure that the shims are replaced correctly. A professional mechanic with a factory shim kit should be able to do it in about two hours.

Changing the camshaft belt

THE CAMSHAFTS OF SOME bikes are driven by toothed belts, which require regular replacement. It is very important that the timing relationship between the crankshaft and the camshaft is not disturbed while the belt is removed and refitted. See your shop manual for specific details.

A toothed camshaft belt

BELT CHANGE

1 REMOVE THE FLYWHEEL

Make sure that the engine is at tdc on the compression stroke and that all timing marks line up. Next, remove the flywheel. You will probably need a special tool for this, but the money saved by not paying a mechanic should cover this expense. On some bikes, it may be necessary to remove various covers before you can get to the flywheel. When removing bolts and screws, push them into a piece of cardboard and label them with the name of the area from which they came as well as the the fitting sequences; this will help during reassembly.

Timing mark

Flywheel

Removal tool

Nut, bolt, and washers from the flywheel

Label bolts and screws pushed into cardboard

2 REMOVE THE TENSIONER

The camshaft belt is held taut by a tensioner. Before you can remove the belt, relieve the tension on it. Do this by disconnecting the tensioner.

3 REMOVE THE CAM BELT

Check again that the alignment of the timing marks is correct before sliding the belt from the pulleys and removing it. Check that the marks *remain* in the correct position during the fitting of the new belt. Make sure that all washers and springs are correctly refitted and that the flywheel is accurately positioned. The flywheel's retaining nut should be very tight.

Two-strokes explained

IN ITS MOST BASIC FORM, a two-stroke engine has only three moving parts – the crankshaft, the connecting rod, and the piston – making it light in weight and cheap to manufacture. Because it fires every revolution, the potential power output is high, but it is not possible for it to have a recirculating lubrication system because the crankcase is used in the combustion process. Instead, the "total-loss" system is employed. The oil is pumped into the crankcases in small quantities and is either burned during the combustion process or expelled with the exhaust gases. On old bikes (and some competition machines without a separate oil pump), the lubricant is mixed with the gas in the fuel tank.

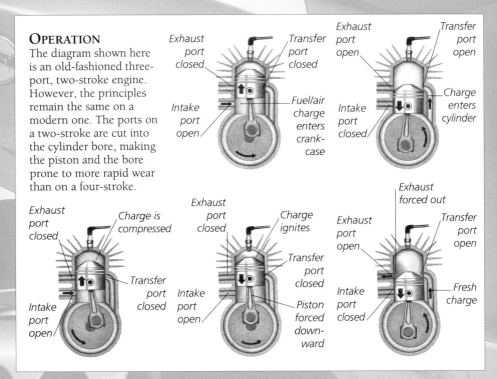

OPERATION

The diagram shown here is an old-fashioned three-port, two-stroke engine. However, the principles remain the same on a modern one. The ports on a two-stroke are cut into the cylinder bore, making the piston and the bore prone to more rapid wear than on a four-stroke.

HOW A TWO-STROKE WORKS

The two-stroke engine carries out the induction, compression, ignition, and exhaust cycle in two strokes of the piston. To achieve this, the incoming charge is sucked into the crankcase as pressure is reduced by the rising piston. The charge is compressed by the falling piston before being forced up ports into the upper cylinder, where it is ignited, forcing the piston down again. This in turn forces fresh fuel mixture into the cylinder, chasing the charge out. This process is repeated over and over. Components in the crankshaft assembly have a shorter life than in four-strokes, and the residues of burned and unburned lubricating oil in the engine and exhaust system can impair the engine's performance.

THE TWO-STROKE ENGINE

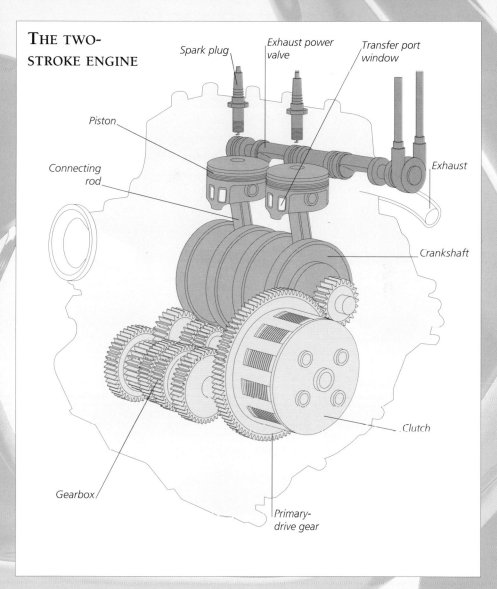

Spark plug

Exhaust power valve

Transfer port window

Piston

Connecting rod

Exhaust

Crankshaft

Clutch

Gearbox

Primary-drive gear

CONTEMPORARY PRACTICE

Although the basic two-stroke engine is mechanically simple, modern engines have many more complex features to enhance their performance. Induction is controlled by reed or rotary valves, and the exhaust timing is varied by a special valve in the exhaust port. The improved performance of modern engines means they produce more heat; therefore, most of them are liquid-cooled. The crankshaft in a two-stroke is normally pressed together and uses ball-bearing big ends. Modern two-strokes have several ports to allow maximum gas flow between the crankcase and the upper cylinder.

Two-stroke components

THE TWO-STROKE ENGINE'S BASIC simplicity means that it requires little in the way of routine maintenance, and a low-power machine should give a long and reliable life. However, high-performance two-strokes are not durable and may require periodic overhauls. In these instances, you will probably have to remove the engine from the frame and substantially or completely dismantle it. This work is beyond the scope of this book, and what follows is for guidance only; consult your shop manual for machine-specific details. One advantage in working on a two-stroke engine is its weight – lifting it onto the workbench won't give you a hernia. The engine's life expectancy can be increased by using good-quality lubricating oil and by warming the engine carefully before hard use.

Piston ring grooves

Transfer port windows

Piston

Retaining clip

Gudgeon pin

Piston rings

Spring ring

PISTON, RINGS, AND CYLINDER

Because of the ports in the cylinder and the piston, these parts wear faster than on four-strokes. Excessive wear will result in a power loss and strange noises. On older engine designs, it is possible to have the cylinder "rebored" to a slightly larger diameter and to fit a correspondingly larger piston. Modern engines use special coatings in the cylinder that don't allow reboring. The cylinder must be replaced or have the coating renewed.

POWER VALVE OVERHAUL

The power valve alters the effective height of the exhaust port, to help the engine work effectively over a wide range of speeds. Unfortunately, because of the conditions it has to work in, the valve can wear severely or become gummed up with oil and carbon. The valve must be kept in optimum condition with regular overhauls for cleaning and seal replacement.

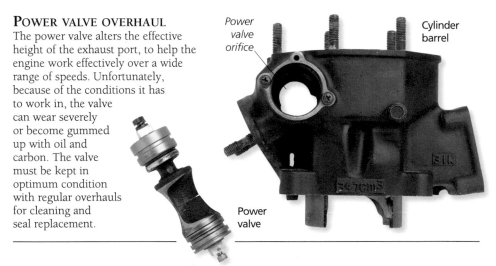

Power valve orifice

Cylinder barrel

Power valve

CRANKSHAFT, BEARINGS, AND SEALS

The two-stroke lubrication system is compromised, and so the crankshaft suffers. Ball or roller bearings are used in the big end, and replacement of these involves pressing the crankshaft apart; this is not a DIY job. Since the crankcases are used in the combustion process, they must be sealed around the crankshaft to prevent loss of compression. Leaking seals result in power loss and an increase in fuel use and engine smoke. If you have dismantled the engine, you must replace the seals.

Crankshaft

Connecting rod

Gudgeon pin

Small-end bearing

Piston

Oil seals

OIL PUMP

It is critical that the correct amount of lubricating oil goes into the engine. As the engine accelerates or runs quickly, it needs more oil than at a constant low speed. The oil pump controls the rate of oil delivery. Adjustment is rarely needed, but may be provided on the control cable or they require that shims be inserted. The oil pump is usually a sealed unit, so if seals within the unit start to leak or if gear teeth break, the pump must usually be replaced.

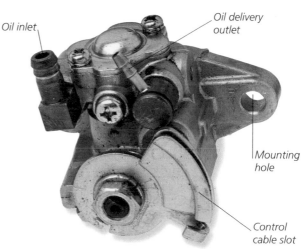

Oil inlet

Oil delivery outlet

Mounting hole

Control cable slot

REED VALVES

Most modern two-strokes feature a reed valve between the carburetor and the crankcase. This is a simple one-way valve that prevents a "blowback" of fuel mixture through the carburetor. The valve's petals are made of steel and the part should last as long as the bike, but inspect it if the engine has been dismantled.

DISC VALVES

Some two-stroke engines use disc valves to control the flow of the fuel mixture into the crankcase, into the side of which the intake port passes. Made of plastic or stainless steel, disc valves are mounted on the end of the crankshaft and, unless damaged by debris entering the engine, should have a long service life.

Ignition explained

THE IGNITION SYSTEM PROVIDES a spark within the cylinder, at exactly the right moment, to ignite the compressed fuel/air mixture. Most modern bikes have maintenance-free electronic ignitions. Apart from keeping leads and connections in good condition, the only maintenance needed is regular inspection, adjustment, and replacement of the spark plugs. Older designs rely on a mechanical switch – the points or contact breaker – to activate the spark. Contact breaker wear affects the spark's timing and quality, so maintenance is crucial for good running.

HOW IGNITION WORKS

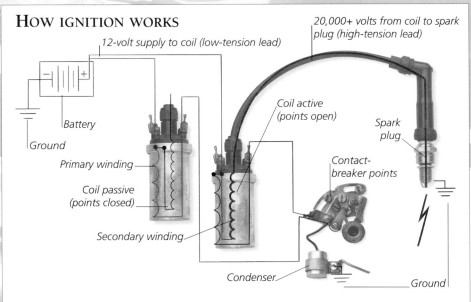

20,000+ volts from coil to spark plug (high-tension lead)

12-volt supply to coil (low-tension lead)

Battery

Ground

Coil active (points open)

Spark plug

Primary winding

Contact-breaker points

Coil passive (points closed)

Secondary winding

Condenser

Ground

HIGH AND LOW TENSION

The ignition spark is created by two interconnected electrical circuits – the low-tension (LT) and high-tension (HT) circuits – and must be upward of 20,000 volts to ignite the fuel mix. The LT circuit provides power and has a mechanical or electronic switch to control the moment at which the spark occurs. The HT circuit comprises a coil, an HT lead, a plug cap, and a spark plug. The coil consists of two separate wire windings. The first carries six or 12 volts through the coil to the points or electronic ignition pickup. When the points open, the

low-voltage current is interrupted, causing a large (HT) voltage to be magnetically induced in the second winding, connected to the plug. This diagram shows the coil twice in order to demonstrate clearly both of its functions. The high-voltage current jumps the gap between the core and the casing (ground) of the plug, creates the spark, and ignites the mixture. Different bikes have different systems: LT power may come directly from the generator or, more commonly, from the battery. Some lightweight bikes have no separate coil; the HT spark is created by a flywheel magneto.

IGNITION COMPONENTS

Well-insulated high-tension lead

Rubber seal

Weather-proof spark plug connector cap

Spark plug

Sealing ring

Porcelain insulation

Thread connects to cylinder head

Insulated core

Ground electrode

Low-tension lead

THE SPARK PLUG
Although modern spark plugs are very reliable, most ignition fault finding begins with the replacement of the spark plug.

THE COIL
Coils come in two types: the cannister coil (above) and the molded coil, in which the windings are mounted on a central core of laminated iron and encased in resin. Both do the same job, and it is important that a coil be replaced by the correct type to ensure complete compatibility with your motorcycle's ignition system.

Points gap screw

Ignition timing screw

Pivot

Eccentric cam

Lubrication pad

THE POINTS
Contact breakers, or points, are controlled by a **cam** that opens them at the critical moment during piston travel. When the points open, the coil emits a high-voltage spark, which is transmitted to the spark plug.

CONTACTS
If your contacts look anything like this, they should have been replaced months ago.

IGNITION PROBLEMS

Because the ignition system's performance is critical to the effective operation of the engine, it is imperative that it works correctly. The modern electronic ignition system is very reliable and almost maintenance-free. Faults in the system, when they do occur, can usually only be rectified by the replacement of (costly) components. Begin any fault-finding session with a thorough check of all connections in the system, and examine wires for breaks or suspect connections. Damp conditions can cause problems, so protect the system with water-repellent spray. The breakdown of insulation in the HT circuit can also cause difficulties. Make sure that spark plug leads and caps are in good condition – they should be replaced every few years. If the problem is still not cured, it must be traced using a multimeter and shop manual.

ELECTRONIC IGNITION
The development of solid-state technology means that mechanical points can now be replaced with a sealed digital unit. This is controlled by magnetic signals from a maintenance-free sensor.

Timing checks and adjustment

MOST MODERN BIKES USE ELECTRONIC ignition, which makes regular timing checks and adjustments unnecessary. Older designs use a mechanical contact breaker (points), which must be correctly set if the engine is to perform properly. See your shop manual for details of this procedure. The guide below may help you understand the process.

RESETTING THE POINTS

Ignition-timing adjuster screw

1 SET THE GAP

The ignition spark occurs when the points are opened by a cam. As the points wear, their gap will change. It must be reset by adjusting the position of the points on their mounting plate using the adjuster screw. With the points in their fully open position, check the gap with a feeler gauge and reset them according to the manufacturer's specification.

2 CHECK THE TIMING

The points must open at exactly the right moment on the engine's ignition stroke. A "static timing check" may be used to check the timing on some machines. In the case shown here, a bulb is connected across the points so that it comes on at the moment when the spark would occur if the engine were running. A special gauge is used to locate the corresponding position of the piston, which is measured in degrees or millimeters before tdc.

3 RESET THE TIMING

The position of the contact breaker mounting plate can usually be changed to alter the timing of the ignition. If there is more than one set of contact breakers (for multicylinder machines), their relationship is also adjustable. This procedure must be done carefully and accurately. If you do not understand it, don't do it yourself. Recheck the timing after completing the task.

CHECKING THE TIMING

The ignition spark occurs before the engine reaches tdc. This allows time for all gases in the cylinder to ignite, so that maximum expansion occurs just after tdc, when maximum pressure is exerted on the piston. When an engine turns slowly, it has more time to burn the fuel mixture in the cylinder than when it turns quickly. To increase engine efficiency, the timing of the spark may be varied according to the speed of the engine. By advancing the ignition, the spark occurs earlier, giving more burning time when the engine is turning quickly. At low speed, the ignition is retarded, allowing smooth running. Modern engines rely on electronics to control the timing, while older designs use a less reliable, mechanical advance/retard system, which requires regular checks.

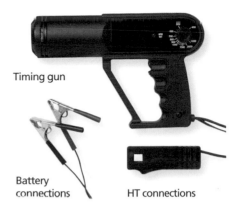

Timing gun

Battery connections

HT connections

USING A TIMING GUN

A static timing check allows the timing to be checked when the engine is not running. To check the timing with the engine running, a timing gun must be used. This is connected to the HT circuit so that it lights up whenever the spark occurs. Special markers on the flywheel and the engine case should be aligned at exactly the moment at which they are illuminated by the gun when the engine is running at a specified speed. If this is necessary, your shop manual will provide details of timing marks and correct engine speeds.

Timing gun

Carburetors explained

THE CARBURETOR MIXES GAS and air to make the fuel vapor on which the engine runs. It also controls how much fuel enters the cylinder, thus dictating the speed and power output of the engine according to throttle position. Carburetors work on the venturi effect (see diagram below). Air is drawn through the venturi and into the engine. At the venturi's base is a small hole (jet) connected to the gas reservoir. The fast-moving air sucks up and vaporizes the gas. A movable needle sits in the jet to regulate the gas flow. The needle is connected to a slide or piston, which is raised or lowered to control engine speed. In a slide carburetor, the position of the slide is controlled by cable from the throttle. In a constant-vacuum (CV) carburetor, the piston is raised or lowered according to a variation of pressure above and below the piston. This is dictated by a throttle-controlled butterfly valve, which restricts the amount of air entering the carburetor. Modern carburetors are complex devices with several jets, valves, and passages, which allow efficient operation over a wide range of openings.

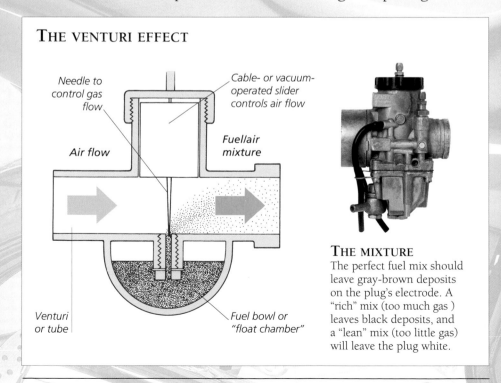

THE VENTURI EFFECT

Needle to control gas flow

Cable- or vacuum-operated slider controls air flow

Fuel/air mixture

Air flow

Venturi or tube

Fuel bowl or "float chamber"

THE MIXTURE
The perfect fuel mix should leave gray-brown deposits on the plug's electrode. A "rich" mix (too much gas) leaves black deposits, and a "lean" mix (too little gas) will leave the plug white.

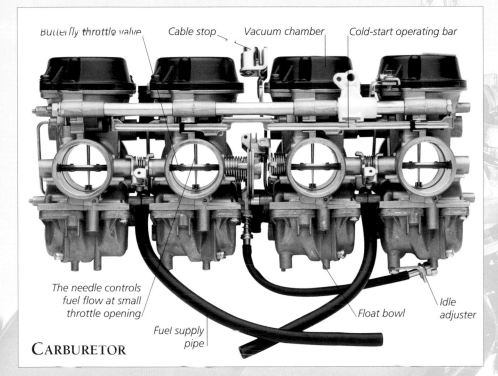

Butterfly throttle valve
Cable stop
Vacuum chamber
Cold-start operating bar

The needle controls
fuel flow at small
throttle opening

Fuel supply
pipe

Float bowl

Idle
adjuster

CARBURETOR

Vacuum
chamber

Float
bowl

CARBURETOR BALANCING

On multicylinder machines, the carburetors
must be synchronized at specific intervals so
that they open at the same time. Carburetor
balancing should be the final stage of a
thorough service and undertaken while the
engine is warm. Two-stroke engines produce
insufficient vacuum to operate a gauge.

CARBURETOR PROBLEMS

Carburetors are delicate instruments that
are sensitive to poor operating conditions and
wear. Carburetors that don't work properly
can cause poor starting, uneven idling, bad
throttle response, coughs, vibration, and
increased fuel consumption. If the carburetors
are out of balance, low-speed performance will
suffer. Dirt in the fuel system causes blocked
jets (see p.46), which stop the carburetor from
working at particular throttle openings. Dirty
air filters make the bike run rich. Air leaks
in the carburetor manifold can make the bike
run lean. Split diaphragm rubbers on CV
carbs can also cause problems, especially on
older bikes, as can incorrectly set float heights.
In case of problems, always start by checking
the fuel supply and the cleanliness of the
carburetor. It can be difficult to differentiate
between ignition and carburetor problems.

Carburetor maintenance

BALANCING THE CARBURETORS on a multicylinder motorcycle can transform the behavior of its engine, which operates best when all the carbs are opening in unison. To perform this job, either a manometer or special, vacuum-operated gauges are required, as are patience and a methodical approach. Many DIY mechanics will happily pass this task on to an experienced technician. Do not adjust anything unless you know what you are doing since it is very easy to get it wrong. Your shop manual will provide machine-specific information.

CARBURETOR BALANCING

1 ACCESS THE CARBURETORS

Before you attempt to balance the carburetors, the bike should be serviced and in good order, especially the ignition and air filters. The float height and the pilot air screws should be correctly set, and the bike must be warm. To gain access to the adjusters, it will probably be necessary to raise the fuel tank. Support it securely and fit an extended fuel line to reach the carbs.

2 FIT THE VACUUM GAUGES

Most bikes have fittings for a manometer or vacuum gauges on the carburetor intake jets, although the type of fitting will vary. Connect the tubes in a logical order. Start the engine and set it to a fast idle using the master-throttle stop screw to get a reading (see your shop manual for this procedure). Be careful not to let the engine overheat during the process; if necessary, turn it off and allow it to cool down periodically. The intention is to get all of the carburetor's cylinders to give a similar reading.

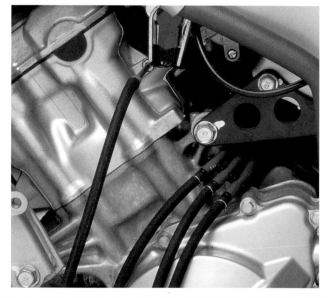

Vacuum gauges
The dials measure the vacuum in the intake manifold. The readings should be the same.

Tube to carburetor_____

3 ADJUST THE SETTINGS

Different machines use different operating systems and require different adjustment techniques (see your owner's manual). Systems in which each carburetor is controlled by a separate cable can be especially tricky. If an operating linkage is fitted, use the carb next to the cable as the master and adjust the others until all the gauges have a similar reading.

4 RESET IDLE SPEED

After setting all the carburetors to the same reading, you must reset the engine idle speed. This is adjusted with either a screw or a knurled knob, and should only be done after the carbs have been balanced. You should make sure that there is enough slack in the cable(s) so that the handlebars can be turned without affecting the engine speed.

FLOAT HEIGHT

The height of the float in the fuel bowl can affect the performance of the carburetor and, although it shouldn't vary, it is worth checking. To do this, you will have to first remove the float bowls. Your shop manual will contain information on the height and measuring technique specific to your bike. While on some carburetors it is possible to adjust the float height by bending the fitting to the float valve, on others the float must be replaced.

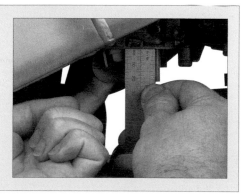

Clutches explained

THE CLUTCH IS A COUPLING between the engine and the gearbox. When disconnected, it permits gear changing and allows the engine to run while the machine is stationary with gear engaged. Most motorcycles use a multiplate clutch, in which a set of friction plates are connected to the engine and another set of plain plates are connected to the gearbox. The two types of plates are fitted alternately within a basket and are forced together by springs. If the springs are compressed – by pulling in the clutch lever – the plates separate and drive is disconnected. Multiplate clutches are usually attached to the gearbox shaft and run in oil, while a few machines use a car-type clutch, which has a single, large friction plate. Manual clutches are operated by a handlebar lever, which is normally connected to the clutch operating arm by cable (in fewer cases, hydraulics are used). Some lightweight machines have automatic clutches attached to the engine. As engine speed is increased by opening the throttle, centrifugal force pushes shoes (similar to drum brake shoes) onto a drum, in order to engage drive.

THE CLUTCH ASSEMBLY

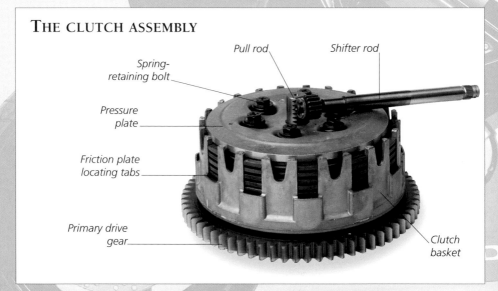

Pull rod

Shifter rod

Spring-retaining bolt

Pressure plate

Friction plate locating tabs

Primary drive gear

Clutch basket

CLUTCH PROBLEMS

The two basic problems from which clutches suffer are clutch slip and clutch drag. Clutch slip occurs when the plates fail to engage together properly and, therefore, the power of the engine cannot be effectively transferred to the gearbox. Clutch slip is usually caused by a lack of free play in the operating mechanism, or by worn plates or springs. Clutch drag – when the plates cannot effectively disengage – leads to poor gear changes or the machine creeping forward when the gear is engaged but the clutch lever is pulled in. It is often caused by excessive free play in the operating mechanism or by a warped disc.

CLUTCH COMPONENTS

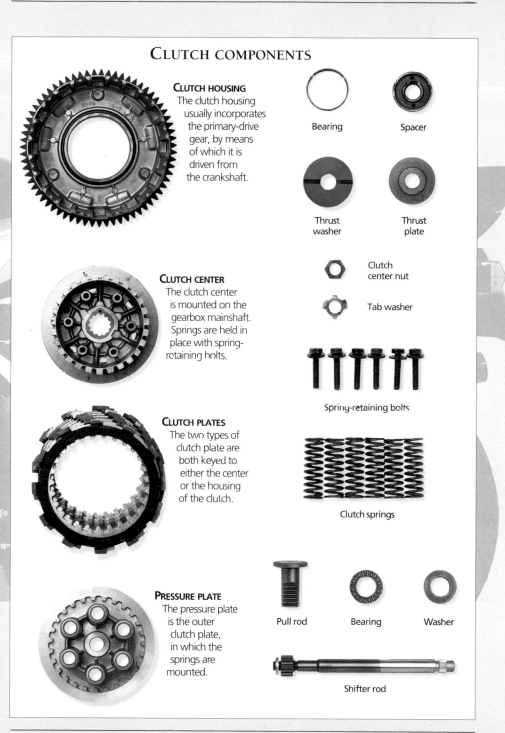

CLUTCH HOUSING
The clutch housing usually incorporates the primary-drive gear, by means of which it is driven from the crankshaft.

Bearing

Spacer

Thrust washer

Thrust plate

CLUTCH CENTER
The clutch center is mounted on the gearbox mainshaft. Springs are held in place with spring-retaining bolts.

Clutch center nut

Tab washer

Spring-retaining bolts

CLUTCH PLATES
The two types of clutch plate are both keyed to either the center or the housing of the clutch.

Clutch springs

PRESSURE PLATE
The pressure plate is the outer clutch plate, in which the springs are mounted.

Pull rod

Bearing

Washer

Shifter rod

Clutch maintenance

UNLESS ABUSED, THE CLUTCH SHOULD have a long and trouble-free life. Maintenance should be limited to occasional adjustment of the operating cable to compensate for wear of the friction material or stretching of the cable. On bikes with hydraulically operated clutches, the system will need periodic bleeding and fluid changes (see p.52). As the friction material becomes more worn, the clutch will gradually become less capable of transferring power without slipping. In time, springs also deteriorate, becoming shorter and losing their strength. Both can be checked by measurement, but the clutch will have to be dismantled in order to do this. Also, clutch plates can warp, which causes the clutch to drag because the plates cannot separate properly.

ADJUSTMENT

A small amount of free play can be adjusted out of the clutch by using the screw adjuster on the handlebar. More adjustment is usually provided at the other end of the cable or at the clutch-operating arm. See your owner's manual for machine-specific details. When no more adjustment is available at the handlebars, return that adjuster to its minimum setting and take up the slack with the other adjuster. See your shop manual for the information necessary to do this task on your machine.

Clutch lever

Screw adjuster

CLUTCH OVERHAUL

In order for you to be able to check for worn or damaged plates and springs, the clutch must be dismantled. It is housed behind an engine case, and access to it will vary between machines. Once you have gained access to it, the clutch can be dismantled. Putting the bike in gear prevents the clutch from turning while you are working on it. Removing the spring-retaining bolts will allow you to remove the springs, the pressure plate, and the other plates for inspection, while leaving the clutch center and housing in place. As always with complicated dismantling, make sure that you make a note of the plates' removal sequence as well as which way around they are fitted. You should also take this opportunity to check the clutch center and housing for signs of wear.

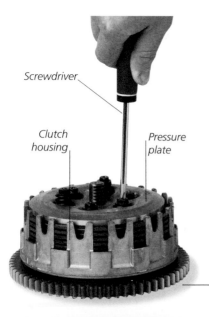

Screwdriver

Clutch housing

Pressure plate

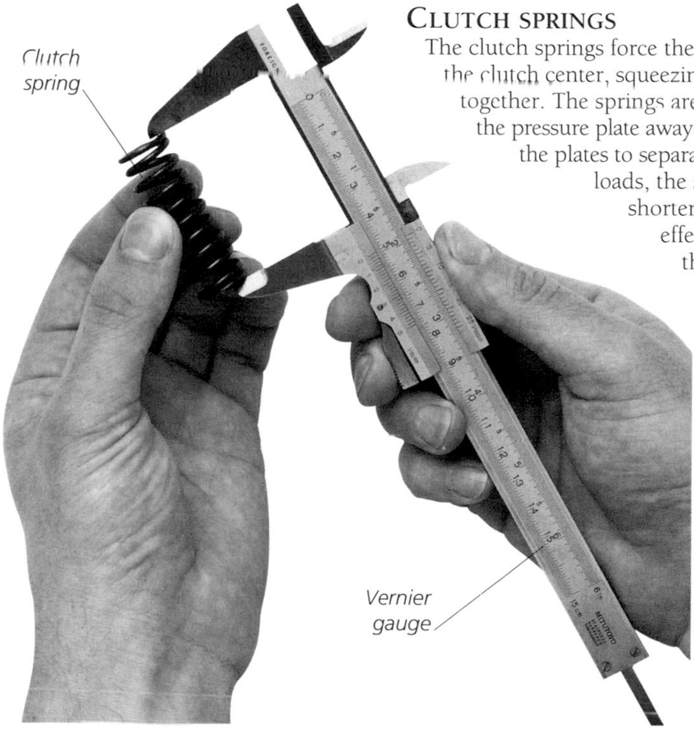

Clutch spring

CLUTCH SPRINGS

The clutch springs force the pressure plate toward the clutch center, squeezing the other clutch plates together. The springs are compressed by forcing the pressure plate away from the center, allowing the plates to separate. Placed under extreme loads, the springs, in time, shorten. This reduces their effectiveness and can allow the clutch to slip.

Whenever the clutch is dismantled, measure the springs to make sure they are within their service limits.

Vernier gauge

Bolt

Clutch spring

CLUTCH PLATES

The clutch's friction plates are subject to wear. You can check that the plates' widths are within the service limits by measuring them with a vernier gauge. If clutch drag is a problem, check that the plates are flat by placing them on a thick piece of flat glass. If they are warped, you should replace them.

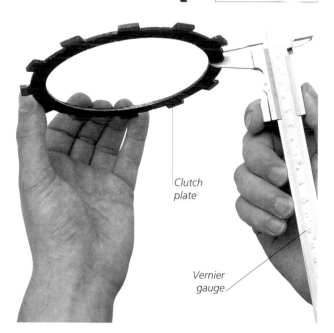

Clutch plate

Vernier gauge

Clutch plates

Suspension problems

THE PERFORMANCE OF THE SUSPENSION components is critical to a bike's good handling. The dampers must operate correctly, and there must be no unwanted play in the suspension. Servicing tasks are limited to oil replacement in telescopic forks and the lubrication of bearings and bushings used in the suspension components. Oil leaks will occur if the seals in the fork or rear suspension unit(s) become worn or damaged. Bearings and bushings in the swingarm and linkage assembly are also prone to wear. This will be accelerated if they are incorrectly lubricated.

FRONT FORK ASSEMBLY

Slider

Cap bolt

Spring seat

Spacer collar

Fork spring

Rebound spring

Damper rod

Dust seal

Retaining clip

Oil seal

Seal spacer

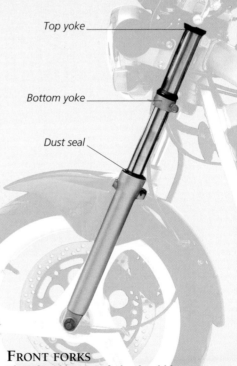

Top yoke

Bottom yoke

Dust seal

FRONT FORKS

The oil in telescopic forks should be replaced every two to three years. If the seals fail, the fork leg must be dismantled to replace them (see pp.88–89). Consult your shop manual for machine-specific details about draining and refilling oil, and for information on the correct grade and quantity of oil required.

REAR SHOCK ABSORBER

SWINGARM UNIT

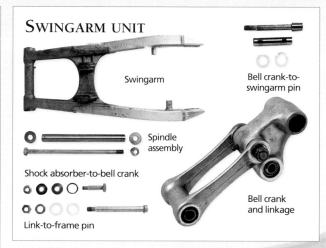

Swingarm

Bell crank-to-swingarm pin

Spindle assembly

Shock absorber-to-bell crank

Link-to-frame pin

Bell crank and linkage

LINKAGE ASSEMBLY

Most bikes with a single suspension unit for the rear suspension will have a connecting linkage between it and the swingarm. The bell crank, linkage, and bearings of the linkage assembly operate under extreme loads and are exposed to road dirt. Bearing failure is almost inevitable if the linkage is not regularly cleaned and lubricated. Some bikes have zinc fittings to allow easy lubrication. However, many do not, making lubrication awkward and inconvenient. It is often ignored, with expensive consequences. If no zinc fittings are present, the assembly should be dismantled, cleaned, and lubricated as often as once a year. The technique for dismantling and reassembling will vary between machines.

Swingarm

SUSPENSION UNIT

As in the case of a telescopic fork, a suspension unit will lose efficiency if the oil leaks or becomes contaminated. However, unlike the telescopic fork, it is almost always impossible for a suspension unit to be overhauled by a DIY mechanic – take it to a specialist instead. If the damper rod, which passes through the seal, is damaged or excessively dirty, seal failure will be considerably accelerated.

SWINGARM BEARINGS

Slight wear on the bearings at the swingarm's pivot will be exaggerated at its wheel end. The uncontrolled movement of the rear axle will have dire effects on the bike's handling. The swingarm bearings should be replaced if wear becomes noticeable. If zinc fittings are present, lubricate the bearings regularly to prolong their life. Different machines use a variety of pivot designs and bearing types. If overhaul is necessary, consult your shop manual for machine specifics.

Front fork overhaul

TELESCOPIC FORKS NEED TO BE dismantled to replace worn seals, but oil changes are quite easy. A plug allows oil to be drained, while new oil is added after removing the top cap. Support the machine under the engine, since removing the fork caps may allow the fork legs to collapse. Although forks are complicated components, a competent DIY mechanic with decent tools and a shop manual should be able to replace the seals on conventional units. With "inverted" forks, a special, expensive tool is needed to fit the new seals. If you can't borrow the tool, it may be more economical for a mechanic to do the job.

FORK OIL REPLACEMENT

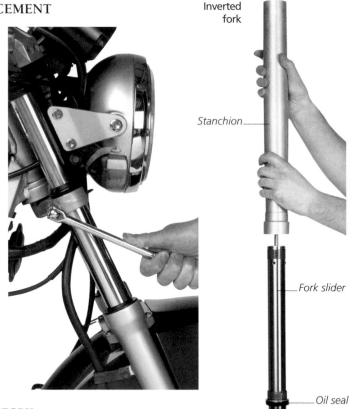

Inverted fork

Stanchion

Fork slider

Oil seal

1 REMOVE THE FORK
The fork leg is clamped to the upper and lower yokes. On some bikes, it is possible to change the seals without removing the complete leg from the yokes. If this is the case, you will still need to support the bike so that the wheel, mudguard, and all extra fittings can be removed. Drain the oil, and loosen any bolts at the top and bottom of the fork legs that secure the damper and the top cap. Loosen the bolts that clamp the fork legs in position on the yokes and you should be able to remove the leg downward through the yokes.

2 DISMANTLE THE FORK
The fork leg unit can now be dismantled in accordance with the instructions in your shop manual. The forks are kept together, and the seals held in place, by a combination of circlips, snap rings, and retaining nuts and screws. Be careful during disassembly and note the positons of all parts that you remove. On conventional forks, the seals must be pried out with a suitable tool; protect the alloy lip of the slider with a small piece of cardboard to avoid damage.

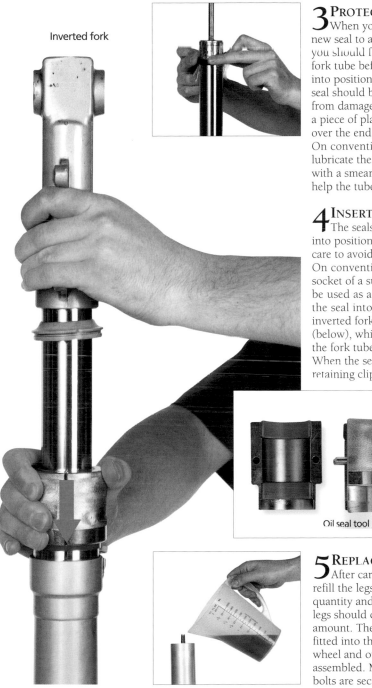

Inverted fork

Oil seal tool

3 PROTECT THE SEAL

When you are fitting a new seal to an inverted fork, you should first lay it over the fork tube before pushing it into position. The lip of the seal should be protected from damage by stretching a piece of plastic sheeting over the end of the tube. On conventional forks, lubricate the lip of the seal with a smear of fork oil to help the tube slide past.

4 INSERT THE SEAL

The seals must be pushed into position evenly and with care to avoid damaging them. On conventional forks, a socket of a suitable size can be used as a drift to ease the seal into position. On inverted forks, a special tool (below), which fits around the fork tube, must be used. When the seal is in place, the retaining clip can be replaced.

5 REPLACE THE OIL

After careful reassembly, refill the legs with the correct quantity and grade of oil. Both legs should contain the same amount. The leg can then be fitted into the yokes and the wheel and other components assembled. Make sure that all bolts are securely tightened.

The unexpected

MOTORCYCLE MAINTENANCE IS ABOUT keeping your bike in the best possible shape so that it never lets you down. But things are never that simple. Inevitably, the bike won't always cooperate. One day it may not start. Or the bolt you want to undo won't budge. Or the one you forgot to tighten falls off. Many simple problems can be solved in the garage, but punctures and dead engines don't wait for a convenient moment to occur. They happen at the worst possible time – you're late, it's raining, and home is a long way away. Coping with these difficulties is a matter of experience and preparation. The quantity of tools you decide to carry with you on the bike will depend on how nervous – or realistic – you are about the chances of a breakdown, and whether you are a member of a roadside-assistance service.

TOOLS FOR SOLVING PROBLEMS

Well-maintained modern bikes should be reliable, so don't get paranoid. However, being able to solve small problems is helpful. Spare nuts, bolts, tape, and cable ties are useful items to keep on hand. More sophisticated repair jobs depend on your ability.

Tire valve tool
If you are fixing a puncture, this tool for removing valve cores is a handy accessory.

Tire valve core

Tire levers
DIY tire fitting is a dying art, but if you are traveling far, tire levers are a sensible precaution. For details on use, see pp.98–99.

Tap and die set
Threaded fasteners get damaged easily but can be restored with either a tap or die.

Tap

Die

Pitch gauge
Normally supplied with a tap and die set, a pitch gauge is used to measure the pitch of a thread.

Fuses
Keep spare fuses for your bike and know where they are located.

Fittings
Deteriorating terminals can cause electrical problems on older bikes.

Fasteners
A well-equipped workshop will have a stock of spare nuts, bolts, and washers.

Cable ties
These little plastic straps help to keep wiring and cables neat on the bike, and are useful aids for roadside repairs.

Soldering iron

1in insulating tape

½ inch insulating tape

Tape
Duct tape can be used to repair everything, while, for electrical repairs, insulating tape is essential.

Bungee cord
This everyday item can be used to hold on a fairing that is about to fall off.

Crimping tool

Duct tape

Multimeter
You will only need this if you are serious about electrical repairs.

Wire-stripping "teeth"

Solder

Multimeter leads

Soldering iron and solder
For electrical repairs, a soldering iron is almost essential. You may be able to borrow one.

Crimping and wire-stripping tool
This tool is used when fitting new terminals or working on electrical wires.

Electrical systems

ELECTRICITY IS USED IN THE motorcycle's ignition system, as well as for powering lights, starter motors, and other components. A complete guide to ohms, volts, capacitators, and resistance is beyond the scope of this book, but the following basics may help you understand what is going on. The specification and type of electrical system fitted will depend on the type of machine. Clearly, a moped doesn't need as comprehensive a system as a superbike but, with some exceptions, the systems are similar. The system can be split into three areas: the generating system, the charging and storage system, and the component circuits. Mopeds and some scooters may omit the storage part.

THE WIRING DIAGRAM

The simplified diagram below shows how the relationship of the parts of a typical electrical system might be arranged. In reality, the system is quite complicated, and the circuit diagram in your owner's manual or shop manual is rather confusing.

KEY		Starter switch wire
Live feeds		Ground
Ignition circuit		Lighting circuit

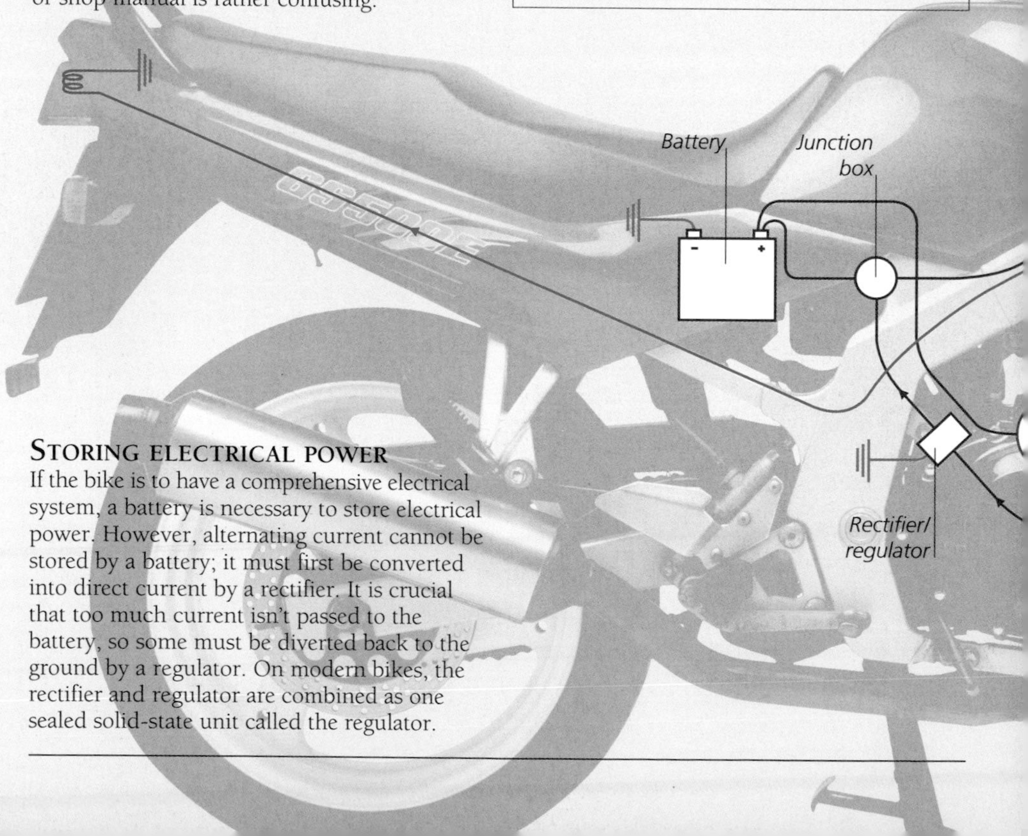

Battery

Junction box

STORING ELECTRICAL POWER

If the bike is to have a comprehensive electrical system, a battery is necessary to store electrical power. However, alternating current cannot be stored by a battery; it must first be converted into direct current by a rectifier. It is crucial that too much current isn't passed to the battery, so some must be diverted back to the ground by a regulator. On modern bikes, the rectifier and regulator are combined as one sealed solid-state unit called the regulator.

Rectifier/ regulator

USING ELECTRICAL POWER

Lights work by transforming electrical energy into heat. The lighting circuits are easy to understand. Power from the positive terminal of the battery is connected to the lightbulb by wires, and returns to the battery via the ground. A switch allows the circuit to be interrupted so that the light can be turned off, but these simple circuits can be made confusing by the presence of warning lights and other complications. Other electrical circuits may be made more difficult to understand by the presence of solid-state components, which control electronic ignition, fuel injection, the regulator, or other functions.

A COMPLETE CIRCUIT

An electrical circuit must be complete for it to work. The component must be connected to the negative and positive terminals of the power source (the battery). To reduce the amount of wires on the bike, the return from the component to the negative terminal of the battery may be made via the (metal) frame of the bike – the ground. If you connect the negative terminal of the battery to the bike's frame and the negative lead from the component to the frame, there is no need to run a separate lead. To make sure that the circuit is complete, good-quality connections to the ground are important.

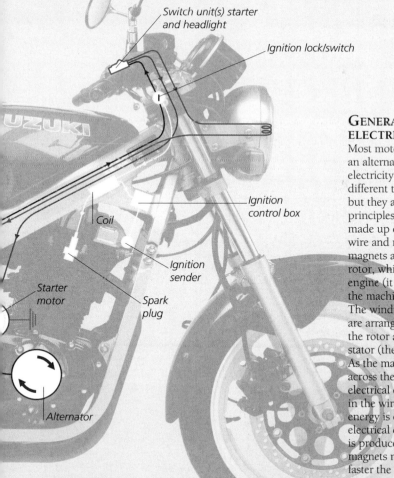

Switch unit(s) starter and headlight

Ignition lock/switch

Ignition control box

Coil

Ignition sender

Starter motor

Spark plug

Alternator

GENERATING ELECTRICAL POWER

Most motorcycles use an alternator to produce electricity. There are several different types of alternator but they all operate on similar principles. An alternator is made up of coils of copper wire and magnets. The magnets are mounted on a rotor, which is turned by the engine (it often doubles as the machine's flywheel). The windings of copper wire are arranged around or within the rotor and are called the stator (they do not move). As the magnetic field moves across the copper stator, an electrical current is induced in the wires and mechanical energy is converted into electrical energy. More power is produced the quicker the magnets move (that is, the faster the engine turns).

Electrical problems

MOST DIY MECHANICS fear electrical problems, but many basic motorcycle faults are relatively easy to locate and repair with very little special equipment. Simple maintenance often prevents problems from occurring. There are only five basic problems – no circuit, a short circuit, no power, too much power, or a faulty

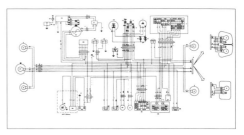

A typical circuit diagram

component – but it's never that easy, since they can all display similar symptoms and you'll need to find one fault among all of the bike's connections, wires, and components. Often, switches can be dismantled for inspection and cleaning, but beware: they can suddenly spring apart, scattering small parts everywhere. A visual check and common sense can be used to find many problems. Identify which parts are relevant to the problem and inspect them, checking connections, wires, and insulation. To go further, you'll need a test light or a multimeter and a wiring diagram. If you are not familiar with using these tools, see a specialist.

ELECTRICAL SYSTEM CHECKLIST

If there is no circuit, check the grounds and switches for corrosion, and check wires and connections for breaks. If you have no power, check the battery, the alternator output, and feeds to and from the battery. Check the alternator and the rectifier if you have too much power. If the circuitry is shorting, check the wiring and the insulation for breaks, and check components, too. When checking for faulty parts, either use a meter or substitute working parts. If you choose the latter, make sure the faulty component is a cause, not a symptom. If the component has been damaged by excess voltage, a new one will be, too, unless the problem is fixed first.

ELECTRICAL MAINTENANCE

CORROSION/DAMPNESS

Prevent moisture penetration with petroleum jelly and water-repellent spray, used sparingly on connectors, terminals, and switches. Corrosion of the terminals or ground connectors also causes problems. Clean corroded connectors with steel wool or sandpaper, and protect them with petroleum jelly.

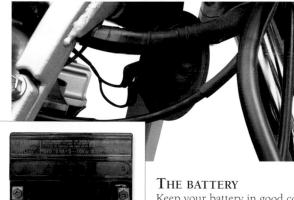

BROKEN WIRES

Examine wires for signs of chaffing and splitting – especially at the steering head, where they are distorted by the steering action, and near sources of heat like the engine and exhaust. Repair splits with good-quality insulating tape or shrink tubing. Correct routing helps prevent damage.

THE BATTERY

Keep your battery in good condition. Replacing it as soon as necessary prevents overworking the alternator and rectifier.

WHAT YOU WILL NEED

For tracing electrical problems, you will need a circuit diagram. You will also need a test light (for simple problems) or, ideally (or for more difficult jobs), a multimeter.

Test light

Test light
It is possible to make a test light using basic components. This one was made from a broken indicator unit.

Terminals and connectors
To prevent recurring problems, repair electrical systems properly. Use quality connectors, tape, and shrink tubing.

Terminals and connectors

COMMON PROBLEMS

•**Blown fuses:** A fuse will blow as a result of a short circuit possibly caused by broken wire, poor insulation, or a faulty component or switch. Which circuit has been activated that caused the fuse to blow? If turning on the left-hand indicator causes the fuse to blow, you can narrow the search to that circuit. Intermittent shorts may occur at the steering head where wires are forced to bend.

•**Blown bulbs:** Bulbs fail with age, but if they blow regularly or are discolored, the cause may be vibration or too much voltage. Check the bulb holder and the light mounting (vibration). Check the battery for signs of overcharging (fluid level low). Have the rectifier and alternator checked, or do it yourself with a multimeter and shop manual.

•**Poor lights:** If the lights are dim but improve as engine revs rise (and the battery is sound), check the condition of the ground between the light unit and the frame.

•**Slow indicators:** If indicators don't function properly when the engine is running slowly (in town) but are all right at speed (on a highway), there may be too much resistance in the circuit. Check grounds, connections, bulbs, and, finally, the flasher unit.

•**A faulty battery:** This will result in an overworked alternator and rectifier. A faulty alternator will result in an undercharged battery. A faulty rectifier will result in either an over- or undercharged battery.

Starting problems

NINETY PERCENT of starting problems can be solved by following a methodical fault-finding system. If the engine is turning over, there are two likely basic reasons why the bike won't start: no spark or no fuel. Don't dismantle the bike until you've checked the obvious, and don't suspect serious problems until you have eliminated the simple ones. If you have been working on the bike, check that area first. If the bike has been standing, replace stale gas. Never try to start the bike with electrical leads disconnected.

ELECTRIC-START BIKE WON'T START

Does the engine turn over properly?   no

yes

KICK-START BIKE WON'T START

Check obvious causes: the kill switch, fuel tap, choke, fuel, sidestand cut-out, and immobilizer.   no

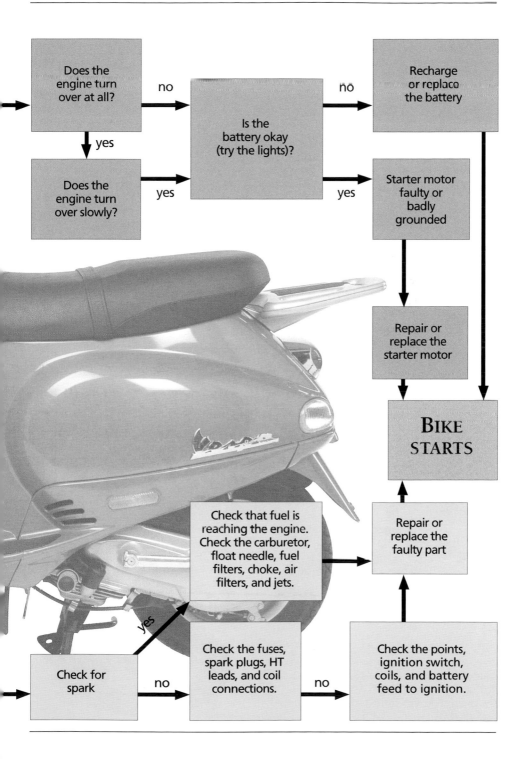

Does the engine turn over at all?

no →

Is the battery okay (try the lights)?

no →

Recharge or replace the battery

yes ↓

Does the engine turn over slowly?

yes →

yes →

Starter motor faulty or badly grounded

↓

Repair or replace the starter motor

BIKE STARTS

Check that fuel is reaching the engine. Check the carburetor, float needle, fuel filters, choke, air filters, and jets.

→

Repair or replace the faulty part

Check for spark

no →

Check the fuses, spark plugs, HT leads, and coil connections.

no →

Check the points, ignition switch, coils, and battery feed to ignition.

yes

Tire and tube removal

CHANGING TIRES CAN BE an awkward job, during which the wheel rim, tire, or inner tube is easily damaged. If you have a performance bike with high-quality tires, get them professionally mounted and balanced. For lightweights, or in an emergency, DIY tire removal and remounting is an alternative. If you have never removed a bicycle tire, practice that before trying a motorcycle tire. Use a puncture repair kit for inner-tube repair and special plugs for tubeless tires.

PUNCTURE REPAIR KIT

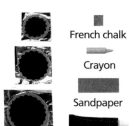

French chalk

Crayon

Sandpaper

Rubber solution

Patches

REMOVING THE TIRE

Valve

1 DEFLATE THE TIRE
Some off-road bikes have a security bolt that you have to loosen and push upward before removing the tire. Also, remove the nut on the valve and, if the tire is not punctured, remove the valve and deflate the tire. Protect the wheel and discs from damage by supporting the rim on wooden blocks or an old tire.

2 BREAK THE BEAD
The tire's two beads must be broken away from the rim before removal can begin. This can be tough, especially on tubeless tires. Try standing on the tire to shift it. When the beads are free, lightly lubricate them with a strong mix of liquid detergent and water – this will help the bead slip over the rim.

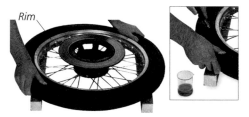

Rim

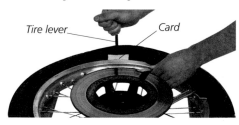

Tire lever   Card

3 LEVER THE TIRE OFF THE WHEEL
Using three tire levers, start near the valve. Protect alloy rims with cardboard. Kneel on the tire opposite the valve and, with two levers about 5in (125mm) apart, lever the tire over the rim. Insert the next lever 5in (125mm) further around and repeat. Remove the center lever and continue until the entire bead is free.

4 PULL THE TUBE FREE
The tube can now be pulled out from the outer cover and repaired or replaced. If it is necessary to remove the tire completely, slide the levers under it and pull the other bead over the rim. Check the insides of both the tire and the wheel rim for damage and potentially damaging, sharp objects.

Tube

5 REPLACE THE TIRE

When replacing the tire, be careful not to trap the tube with the levers. Work toward the valve, which can be pushed upward into the tire as the levers are used to complete the final section. Lightly brushing a solution of liquid detergent onto the bead will help it slide on. Having mounted the tire to the wheel, inflate the tire to seat the beads correctly. The solution of liquid detergent may help them to slide on evenly. If you have completely removed the tire, make sure that you refit it with the rotational arrow pointing in the correct direction.

Lever

Spray to fix
Emergency puncture repairs can be done by filling the tire with a special spray foam.

TUBELESS TIRE REPAIR

Punctures in tubeless tires can usually be repaired using plugs that must be inserted from the inside of the tire. This job is best done by a professional. "Get you home" repairs can sometimes be done using plugs that are inserted from the outside while the tire is still in place. The plugs are part of a tubeless tire repair kit that contains everything necessary to carry out the repair, including instructions. However, even a successful roadside repair should only be temporary. Restrict your speed while it is in place, and do a full repair as soon as possible.

TIRE REPAIR KIT

Chalk

Plugs

Awl/insertion tool

Rubber solution

Knife

Air canister adaptor

Air canister

WHEEL BEARINGS

If badly lubricated or exposed to dirt, wheel bearings can fail. Removal and replacement require care and ingenuity. Remove dust seals and retaining clips, then, working evenly and gently with a suitable drift and hammer, tap the bearing out from the opposite side of the wheel – it should come out squarely. Squeeze new bearings carefully into position, applying pressure to their outer race with a suitable spacer. Bearings for use with single-sided swingarms must be fitted according to the manufacturer's instructions.

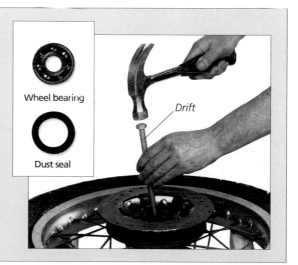

Wheel bearing

Dust seal

Drift

Nuts and bolts

YOU WILL FIND AN ASSORTMENT of threaded fasteners joining the components on your motorcycle and, unless your bike is a Harley-Davidson or is very old, it will use a metric thread system. (Harley uses an American thread that requires imperial A/F – across flat – tools, which are not discussed here.)

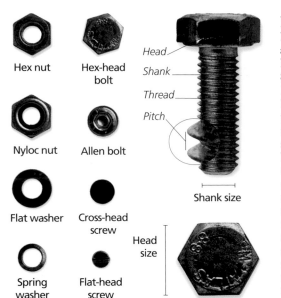

Hex nut

Hex-head bolt

Nyloc nut

Allen bolt

Flat washer

Cross-head screw

Spring washer

Flat-head screw

Head

Shank

Thread

Pitch

Shank size

Head size

BOLT SIZES

Most bolts have either a hex head or an Allen head. The most common head sizes on conventional bolts are 8mm, 10mm, 11mm, 12mm, 13mm, 14mm, 17mm, 19mm, and 22mm. Different manufacturers have different preferences. Each head size corresponds to a different shank size, and it is the shank size that is used to specify the bolt. A 10mm hex head (5mm Allen) corresponds to an M6 bolt, while a 13mm hex head (6mm Allen) corresponds to an M8 bolt. The pitch of the bolt – that is, the width of its thread – is also important. An M6 bolt normally has a 1mm pitch and is specified as M6 x 1.00. Two bolts may appear to be the same size, but if their pitches differ, any attempt to swap them over will damage the threads.

REPAIRING THREADS

Screw and bolt threads, especially those in alloy casings, are easily damaged. Lightly damaged threads can be repaired using a tap or die. Serious damage can usually only be repaired by having a special insert fitted professionally.

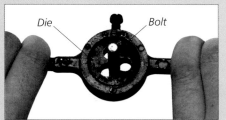

Die

Bolt

TAP

A tap is used for restoring internal threads. Make sure that it is the correct size and thread form, and that you fit the tap into the true thread.

DIE

The die is turned around the thread like a nut. Again, you should make sure that it is correctly fitted to the thread to avoid causing further damage.

Accident damage

PLASTIC PANELS FITTED TO MOTORCYCLES are fragile. Even following (inevitable) low-speed drops, replacement or professional repair is the only way to achieve a decent cosmetic finish. However, there are ways of making a lightly damaged panel visibly acceptable, unless under close scrutiny, as well as serviceable.

ADHESIVES

Careful application of superglue can rejoin cracks in some types of plastic. Unfortunately, it is a brittle repair and may crack again. Back up the repair with duct tape or epoxy resin on the back side of the panel.

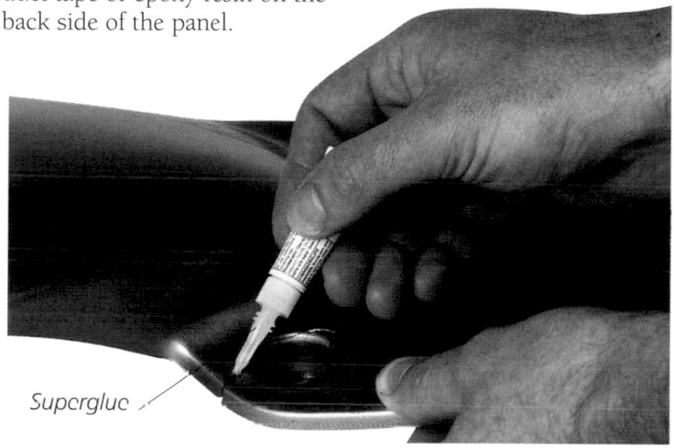

Superglue

ADHESIVES

Superglue and removal fluid

EPOXY RESIN

Mix epoxy adhesive with its hardener for lasting results.

PLASTIC WELDING

Special equipment is available for repairing plastic panels, but DIY mechanics usually make do with an electrical soldering iron, carefully used on the back of the panel to rejoin cracks. Be careful not to overheat the plastic, and back up the repair with duct tape. Don't inhale the fumes.

Soldering iron

Bike panel

Maintenance chart

REGULAR MAINTENANCE IS ESSENTIAL to keep your bike running well, to stop problems from starting, or to locate them early. The amount of maintenance your bike will require depends on the type of use and how much use it gets. For example, many short trips will cause more wear than one long trip, while use in winter causes more wear than use in summer. Make sure you adjust your maintenance schedule accordingly. Treat the chart below as a guide, but you should also check the specific service intervals in your owner's manual. Check your bike over well, and adjust where necessary, before any long trip. Also remember, if you take the bike off the road for long periods of time, its condition may deteriorate unless preventive precautions are taken. Clean it, lubricate it, disconnect the battery, and drain the fuel from the carburetor before putting it away. While the motorcycle is out of action, you should periodically turn the engine over. Proper maintenance should ensure that your motorcycle gives many miles of trouble-free service and satisfaction.

HOW OFTEN SHOULD I CHECK?

Follow the color coding (right) in the chart below, which gives an approximate indication of check regularity. The symbol "**2/3**" beside an annual check means "Every 2–3 years."

☐ WEEKLY CHECK

☐ MONTHLY CHECK

☐ ANNUAL CHECK

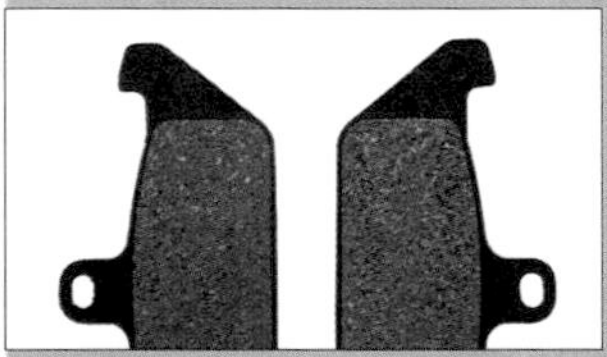

BRAKES
- Check/adjust/lubricate drum brake controls ☐
- Check pad shoe wear ☐
- Check hose connection/leaks ☐
- Bleed hydraulic operating system   2/3 ☐
- Change hydraulic fluid ☐

CARBURATION
- Check/adjust idle speed ☐
- Check/adjust/lubricate throttle/choke cable ☐
- Balance carburetors ☐
- Check/clean air filter ☐
- Replace air filter   2/3 ☐
- Check fuel lines and clean fuel filters ☐

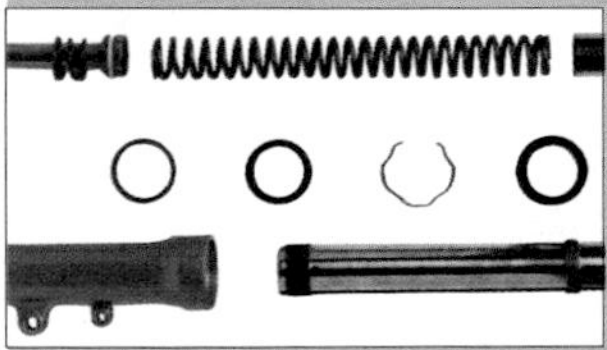

CHASSIS AND SUSPENSION
- Check nuts and bolts ☐
- Check for oil leaks ☐
- Check swingarm bearings and linkage ☐
- Lubricate swingarm bearings ☐
- Check steering-headrace bearings   2/3 ☐
- Change front fork oil ☐

COOLING SYSTEM
- Check coolant level ☐
- Inspect radiator hoses ☐
- Replace coolant 2/3 ☐

ELECTRICAL
- Check lights ☐
- Check brake-light switch ☐
- Check battery fluid level and condition ■
- Check wiring condition ☐

ENGINE
- Check/adjust tappets (four-strokes)
- Change cam belt (some four-strokes)
- Check cam chain tension (if appropriate)
- Inspect two-stroke cylinder/head/exhaust
- Check nuts and bolts ■

IGNITION
- Check spark plug gap and condition ☐
- Check leads/spark plug caps ☐
- Replace spark plug
- Check/adjust contact breakers (if appropriate)

LUBRICATION
- Check engine oil level ☐
- Change oil
- Change filter
- General lubrication (including cable check) ■
- Check oil pump and hoses (two-strokes) ☐
- Check/change transmission oil

TRANSMISSION
- Check/adjust/lubricate chain ☐
- Check/adjust/lubricate clutch cable ☐
- Check gearbox/drive shaft oil level (if appropriate)
- Change gearbox/drive shaft oil (if appropriate)
- Check drive belt (on belt-driven bikes) ■

TIRES AND WHEELS
- Check tire pressure/condition ☐
- Check spokes/wheel rims ■
- Check wheel bearings ☐

Glossary

Air cooling The use of air to reduce temperature.

Air filter A filter, usually of paper or foam, that prevents dirt and dust from entering the carburetor.

Alternating current An electrical current that regularly reverses (alternates) direction.

Alternator An electrical generator that produces alternating current.

Ampere A unit for measuring electrical current. The ampere/hour rating of a battery refers to the amount of current that the battery can discharge for a ten-hour period. An 18Ah battery can supply 1.8 amperes for ten hours.

Bdc (bottom dead center) The point during crankshaft rotation at which the piston is in its lowest possible position.

Bead Part of a tire that is shaped to fit the rim. It is made from a steel wire inside the tire casing.

Belt drive A system of power transmission using a belt. On motorcycles, this is normally a toothed rubber belt used for driving the camshafts or the final drive.

Bevel gears A pair of gears with faces cut at an angle of 45°, allowing drive to be turned through 90°.

Big end The larger (crankshaft) end of the connecting rod.

Bike stand A tool used to raise a bike's rear wheel off the ground. Similar stands are also available for front wheels.

Bottom out The point at which a spring is fully compressed. The term used for the oppposite state, when the spring is fully extended, is "top out."

Box wrench A wrench that fits all six flat edges of a nut. It is usually turned with a bar.

Brake caliper A unit, containing pistons and pads, that grips the brake disc to slow it. Usually it is hydraulically operated.

Bucket A cam lifter shaped like a bucket.

Cam An eccentric rotor that converts rotational movement into linear movement. Cams are used in the operation of valves, contact breaker points, and drum brakes.

Cam lifter The component that rests on the lobe of the camshaft and transfers reciprocating movement to the valve, rocker, or pushrod.

Camshaft A shaft with two or more cams used

in the four-stroke engine to operate intake and/or exhaust valves.

Camshaft belt An endless belt used to transfer power from the crankshaft to the camshaft.

Carburetor The device that mixes fuel and air into combustible vapor.

"C" clip A sprung C-shaped clip that fits in a groove on a shaft. The shaft passes through the center of the "C."

Centrifugal clutch A clutch system used on some lightweight bikes that operates by using centrifugal force – throwing outward when rotated. As engine speed increases, rotating shoes are thrown against the inside of a drum, which transfers power to the transmission.

Circlip A special retaining clip that fits around (external) a shaft or inside a hole (internal). It is fitted or removed with special circlip pliers.

Clutch A device that disengages the drive between the engine and the transmission.

Collar A separate part of a tubular or cylindrical component that fits around it and may provide a means of adjustment or restraint.

Compression Squeezing something (springs or a gas, for example) into a smaller space.

Compression stroke The stroke of the piston that compresses the fuel mixture in the cylinder.

Constantly variable transmission (CVT) A variable-ratio, automatic transmission system used on scooters and mopeds.

Constant loss See *Total loss.*

Contact breaker The sprung switch in the low-tension ignition circuit that controls the timing of the spark in the high-tension circuit. Contact breakers are operated by a cam and are sometimes called "points." Modern systems controlled electronically do not need this feature.

Crankcases The lower cases of the engine that house the crankshaft.

Crankshaft The cranked shaft in an engine that changes the piston's linear motion into rotational motion.

"C" spanner wrench A wrench for turning collars and castellated nuts. The "C" fits around the collar, while a tooth at one end of the "C" fits a slot in the collar.

Cush drive A shock absorber for the transmission system. Usually a rubber cushion in the rear hub.

CVT See *Constantly variable transmission.*

Cylinder A tube in which a piston usually moves up and down.

Cylinder head A casting that caps the cylinder. It contains the combustion chamber, the spark plug, and, in a four-stroke, the valves.

Damper A device that controls the speed of steering or suspension movement.

Degreasant A substance that loosens oily dirt so that it can be washed off.

Direct current Electrical current that flows in one direction only.

Drain plug/drain screw A screw that, when it is removed, allows liquid to be drained from a container.

Dry sump A four-stroke lubrication system in which oil is stored in a separate tank rather than in the engine sump.

Dynamo An electric generator that produces direct current.

Earth The part of an electrical circuit that returns to source (usually the negative terminal of the battery) via the frame.

Eccentric An elipse or a wheel that rotates, but not around its center.

Electrodes Metal parts in a spark plug between which the spark jumps.

Endless chain A chain that has no split link. It must be fitted without being broken.

Fairing An enclosure fitted to improve a bike's aerodynamics and/or rider comfort.

Feeler gauges Thin metal strips of specified thicknesses used for the accurate measurement of small gaps.

Filament The wire inside a light bulb, which glows when passing current.

Final drive A means of transmitting power to the driven wheel, usually by chain, shaft, or belt.

Float bowl The fuel reservoir for the carburetor. Fuel flow is controlled by a valve operated by a float. Also called "float chamber."

Float charger A special type of charger used to recharge maintenance-free batteries.

Float height The height at which the float closes the float valve.

Float valve A float-operated valve that stops the flow of liquid into the reservoir when the level reaches a certain height.

Flywheel A metal rotor attached to the crankshaft that helps to smooth the engine's power delivery.

Four-stroke An engine operating cycle in which there is a power stroke for every four strokes of the piston. For a more detailed explanation, see pp.64–65.

Free play The free movement in components or a control mechanism before resistance is felt. It may or may not be desirable.

Friction Resistance to the free movement of surfaces/bodies in contact with one another.

Gearbox The housing for the gear pinions and selectors, although it normally refers to the complete assembly.

Gear ratio The ratio of reduction achieved by a pair of gears. The smaller gear (pinion) turns more than the larger gear.

Gears Mechanical devices that transmit power and turning motion from one shaft to another. They operate in pairs and usually take the

form of wheels with teeth that mesh together.

Grease A semisolid lubricating oil.

Halogen A gas used in some bulbs to enhance filament regeneration.

Housing An instrument unit.

Hub The wheel's center.

Ignition The moment when the fuel/air mixture is ignited, or the system that ignites it.

Ignition timing The point at which, relative to crankshaft rotation or piston position, the ignition spark occurs.

Inverted forks Telescopic forks in which the lower section, where the wheel is mounted (slider), telescopes into the fixed upper tube (stanchion). Inverted forks are sometimes known as "upside-down forks."

Jet A calibrated hole through which gas, oil, or air passes.

Kinetic energy The energy of movement.

Linear movement Movement in either direction on a single axis.

Liner A sleeve of harder material within a component.

Liquid cooling An engine cooling system that uses liquid (normally water-based).

Lubricant A substance that reduces friction between rubbing surfaces.

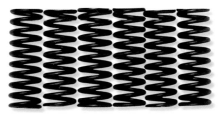

Magneto A high-tension spark generator for the ignition system, with no external power source.

Manometer An instrument for measuring the pressure of gases.

Monograde oil An oil with a single viscosity.

Moped A pedal-assisted bike of less than 50cc.

Mounting lug The small projection from a component by which it is bolted to another part.

Multigrade oil An oil that performs with varying viscosity according to the temperature.

O ring A circular rubber seal.

O-ring chain A chain that contains lubricant, which is kept in place by O rings, within its rollers.

Owner's manual A set of operating instructions and basic maintenance information supplied with new machines.

Petroleum jelly A semisolid substance made up of wax and petroleum.

Pilot air screw The carburetor adjustment screw that alters the ratio of air in the fuel/air mix at zero or minimal throttle openings.

Piston A component that fits inside a cylinder and transmits pressure changes.

Pivot The pin or shaft on which something turns.

Points See *Contact breaker.*

Polarity The negative or positive quality of an electrical terminal that determines the direction a current will flow.

Primary drive A system of transferring power from engine to gearbox, usually by chain or gear.

Pulley The wheel used for changing the direction of a belt's travel or power transference to the belt.

Pushrod A rod used in ohv (overhead valve) engines and some clutches to transfer linear force.

Ratchet A mechanism that only allows turning motion in one direction.

Ratio The relationship (in terms of quantity) of one thing to another when used together.

"R" clip A sprung clip in the shape of a capital "R." Often used in axles instead of a split pin.

Riveted-link chain A chain connected by a riveted link rather than a spring clip.

Rectifier An electrical device used for converting alternating current into direct current by passing it in one direction only.

Regulator Device for controlling alternator output, to prevent excess voltage.

Rotational movement Circular movement around an axis.

Rotor A rotating component.

Scooter A small-wheeled utilitarian machine with a step-thru frame.

Shaft A rotating rod on which gears are mounted or that transfers power.

Shim A thin piece of metal (which may be of a specified thickness) used to adjust the position or the relative thickness of another component.

Shock absorber A device for smoothing irregularities such as the cush drive in the transmission. Also used to describe a suspension unit comprising a spring and damper.

Shoe A rigid component that is pressed against a rotating component to create friction. Normally, a special type of friction material is fitted to the sole.

Shop manual A comprehensive manual of information and instruction about how to repair and maintain a specific model of motorcycle.

Side valve A valve at the side of a cylinder.

Slack See *Free play.*

Sleeve A means of reducing or restoring the internal diameter of a tube, hole, or cylinder.

Slider A part that moves in a sliding motion, such as the lower component of a fork leg.

Small end The piston end of the connecting rod.

Soft link A special link for joining chains, riveted together with a special tool. It is more practical than an endless chain and stronger than a spring clip.

Spark plug A component that screws into the engine's cylinder head. It contains the electrodes across which the ignition spark jumps.

Splines Grooves on either a shaft or the component that fits to it. When mated, the two parts lock together.

Split link A removable link, which is retained by a spring clip, used for joining a chain.

Split pin A security pin that fits through a hole in a shaft or bolt. It is split so that the emerging end can be bent in two directions to prevent it from coming out of position.

Spoke The part of the wheel that connects the rim to the hub.

Spring clip A metal retaining device, the natural shape of which must be distorted in order to release it.

Sprocket Toothed wheel on which a chain runs.

Stanchion A strong upright member. The part of a telescopic fork leg that does not move.

Stator The part that remains static.

Step-thru A frame layout with a low structure between the seat and the steering head.

Stroke The measurement of the length of piston travel in the bore, usually expressed in millimeters.

Sump The reservoir for lubricating oil at the bottom of an engine.

Suspension The system of springs and dampers that isolates the main part of the machine from the wheels' movement.

Swingarm A suspension member pivoted at one end and supporting the wheel at the other. In most cases, the swingarm is more accurately described as a pivoted fork, since the wheel is supported at both sides.

Tachometer An instrument that measures engine speed, calibrated in revolutions per minute.

Tdc (top dead center) The point at which the crankshaft and piston are in their highest possible positions.

Telescopic forks A front suspension system with two legs. Each has sliding and fixed tubular parts that telescope together to allow movement.

Terminal The fitting on an electrical component to which an electrical connection is made.

Thermostat A device that automatically controls the cooling system's temperature. It usually has a temperature-sensitive component that regulates the flow of liquid to or from the radiator.

Throttle A device that controls engine speed by restricting the flow of air and fuel into the engine.

Timing The measurement of the moment at which valves open or close, or when the spark occurs. It is normally expressed in

degrees or millimeters before or after tdc or bdc.

Timing chain The chain that connects the crankshaft to the camshaft(s).

Timing marks Marks indicating the position of the camshaft and/or crankshaft.

Toothed belt A flexible reinforced belt with teeth on its inside surface to allow correct positioning. It can be used to connect two rotating components, which must work in synchronization.

Torque Twisting or turning force.

Torque arm A solid connection that prevents an object that would naturally turn from doing so. In brakes, the torque arms prevent the caliper or brake plate from turning with the wheel as the brake is applied.

Total loss An ignition or lubrication system in which electricity or oil is used without being generated or recirculated.

Trail bike A dual-purpose motorcycle that

can be used in on- or off-road situations.

Transmission A collective term for the several components that are responsible for transmitting power from the machine's engine to its driving wheels.

Two-stroke An engine operating cycle in which there is a power stroke for every two strokes of the piston. See pp.70–71 for a full description.

V belt A rubber belt that, in section, is a "V" shape.

Venturi The main carburetor passage through which air is sucked and which, in turn, sucks up and vaporizes the gas as it passes (a process known as the venturi effect).

Vernier gauge A tool used for the accurate measurement of internal and external dimensions.

Viscosity The thickness, and therefore resistance to flow, of a liquid. An important part of an oil's specification, it is shown by an SAE number: the higher the figure, the thicker the oil.

V-twin A two-cylinder engine layout in which the cylinders form a "V" shape.

Wet sump A lubricating system used in four-stroke engines in which the oil is stored in the engine sump.

Wheel alignment The relationship between the front and rear wheels.

Index

A

access panels, removal
34
accidental damage,
repairing 101
adhesives, bodywork
repairs 101
air box 45
air cooling, engines 12
air filters 45, 78
Allen wrenches 14, 38
alloy, polishing 36
alternating current 92
alternators 93, 94, 95
antifreeze 19
automatic transmission,
scooters 13
axle nuts
loosening 24
removing wheels
26, 27
axles
adjusting drive chain
25
removing wheels 26
wheel alignment 59

B

batteries 92
electrical circuits 93
problems 95
filling up and
recharging 23
bearings
steering-head 60, 61
suspension linkage
61, 87
swingarm 60, 87
two-stroke engines 73

wheels 61, 99
belt drive 54
bike stands 26, 56, 58
big end 73
bleeding hydraulic fluid
52
bodywork
cleaning 36–7
removal 34–5
repairs 101
bolts 100
loose 28
brake fluid, leaks 28
brake pads 48, 49
replacing 50–1
brakes 48–53
adjusting levers 17
adjusting pedal angle
16
brake-light switches
20
checking 50–1
free play adjustment
17
hydraulics 19, 52
maintenance chart 102
removing wheels 27
replacing pads and
shoes 50–1
storing bikes 37
brushes 37
bucket-and-shim valve
trains 66, 68
bungee cords 91

C

"C" spanner wrenches
15, 39
cables

cable ties 91
clutch 84
free play adjustment
17
lubrication 41, 53
calipers, brake 49
cam lobes 65, 66
camshafts
changing belt 69
drive chains 67
four-stroke engines
65, 66
carburetors 46, 78–81
balancing 79, 80–1
draining 37
float height 80, 81
maintenance chart 102
problems 79
two-stroke engines 73
chain link breakers 38
chains see drive chains
chamois leather 37
chassis
cleaning 36–7
maintenance chart 102
chrome, polishing 36
circuit diagrams 92,
94, 95
cleaning 36–7
clips, loose 28
clutch 54, 82–5
cable lubrication 53
components 83
free play adjustment
17
hydraulics 19
maintenance 84–5
problems 82
coils, ignition 75

combination spanner
wrenches 38
compression
suspension 31, 33
two-stroke engines 73
constant-vacuum (CV)
carburetors 78, 79
constantly variable
transmission 55
contact breakers, ignition
74, 75, 76
cooling system
coolant check and
fill-up 19
leaks 28
maintenance chart 103
copper grease, spark
plugs 47
corrosion 36
electrics 94
crankcases
sight windows 18
two-stroke engines
70, 73
crankshafts
four-stroke engines 64
two-stroke engines
70, 73
crimping tool 91
cush drive 27, 55
custom bikes 12
cylinder heads,
four-stroke engines
64, 66
cylinders
four-stroke engines
64, 66
ignition 74
two-stroke engines 72

D

dampers 30–1
  adjusting 33
  problems 86
degreasant 36
detergents 36, 37
dies, repairing threads 100
dipsticks, oil 18
direct current 92
disc brakes 16, 48–9
  replacing pads 50–1
disc valves, two-stroke engines 73
drive chains 24–5, 54
  camshafts 67
  chain and sprocket replacement 56–7
  checking tension 24
  lubrication 25, 36
  maintenance 25
drive shafts, oil 41
drive systems 55
drum brakes 16, 49
  removing wheels 27
  replacing shoes 51
dry-sump engines 41, 42
duct tape 91

E

electrical system 92–5
  checklist 94
  circuit diagrams 92, 94, 95
  circuits 93
  fuses 21
  ignition 74
  maintenance chart 103
  problems 94–5
electronic ignition 74, 75
engines see four-stroke

engines; two-stroke engines
epoxy resin 101
extension bars, spanner wrenches 15

F

faired headlights 22
fairings, removal 34–5
fasteners 91
feeler gauges 14, 63
  bucket-and-shim adjustment 68
  screw-and-locknut adjustment 67
fenders, removal 35
filters
  air 45, 78
  fuel tank 46
  oil 42–3
final-drive chain 54
float bowls, carburetors 46, 81
"float chargers," batteries 23
float height, carburetors 80, 81
floating-caliper disc brakes 49, 51
flywheel magnetos 74
flywheels, removing 69
four-stroke engines
  air cooling 12
  maintenance 67–9
  maintenance chart 103
  oil 18, 40, 42
  operation 64–6
  sumps 41
free play adjustment 17
front forks 31
  adjusting preload 32

components 86
  oil replacement 86
  overhaul 88–9
front wheels, removal 26, 27
fuel
  carburetor 78
  leaks 28
fuel tank
  draining 37, 46
  filters 46
  removal 35
funnels, greaseproof paper 53
fuses 21, 91, 95

G

gear levers, adjusting 16
gearboxes 54
  clutches 82–5
  drive chain 24
  oil 41
  oil change 44
grease guns 39
greaseproof paper funnels 53

H

halogen bulbs 21
handlebars
  adjusting levers 16
  steering-head bearings 60
headlights
  bulbs 21, 22
  faired headlights 22
high-tension (HT) circuit 74
hydraulics 19
  bleeding hydraulic fluid 52

clutches 84
  leaks 28

I

idle speed, resetting 81
ignition 74–7
  components 75
  maintenance chart 103
  problems 75
  spark plugs 47
  timing checks and adjustment 76–7
impact drivers 62
indicators
  lenses 22
  problems 95
inflating tires 29
insulating tape 91

L

leaks 28
  hydraulic fluid 52
lenses, indicators 22
levers, greasing 41
lightbulbs 20, 22, 95
lights 20–2
  brake lights 20
  bulbs 20, 22, 95
  electric 93
  headlights 21, 22
  problems 95
  rear lights 22
linkage, suspension 61, 87
liquid-cooled engines 71
  coolant 19
  loose bolts 28
low-tension (LT) circuit 74
lubrication 18–19, 40–1
  brake shoes 51

cables 53
drive chain 25
gearboxes 44
maintenance chart 103
oil changes 42–4
suspension linkage 87
tools 39

M
magnetos 74
maintenance chart
102–3
mallets 39
manometers 80
manuals 15, 38
marine grease 37
middleweight machines
8–9
mopeds
electrical system 92
transmission 54, 55
multigrade oils 40
multimeters 91

N
nuts 100
loose 28

O
O-ring chains 25, 54
offset, wheel alignment
59
oil
changing 42–3
checking levels 18
disposal 42
drive shafts 41
filters 42–3
four-stroke engines
40, 42
front fork overhaul

88–9
gearboxes 41, 44
leaks 28
suspension 31
two-stroke engines
40, 42, 70
types 40
viscosity 40
oil-impregnated foam
filters 45
oil pumps, two-stroke
engines 73
oil seal tools 62, 89
opposed-piston caliper
brakes 49, 50
owner's manuals 15

P
paintwork, polishing 36
panels, repairs 101
pedals, greasing 41
petroleum jelly 37, 94
pilot air screws,
carburetor 80
pin spanner wrenches 15
pistons
four-stroke engines 64
suspension 31
two-stroke engines
70, 72
pitch gauges 90
pivot points, lubrication
36
plastic welding 101
pliers 14, 38
points, ignition 74,
75, 76
polish 36, 37
power valves, two-stroke
engines 72
power washers 37

preload, suspension
30, 32
pressure, tires 29
pressure gauges 14
pressure plate, clutch 83
pullers 63
pumps
inflating tires 29
oil 73
puncture repair kits 98
punctures 99

Q
"quickly detachable"
(QD) rear hubs 27

R
rear lights, changing
bulbs 22
rear shock absorbers 87
rear wheels, removal 26
reboring cylinders 72
rectifiers 94, 95
reed valves, two-stroke
engines 73
regulators 92
ring spanner wrenches
15
rod-operated rear
brakes 17
rust 36

S
scooters 8, 13
electrics 92
removing wheels 27
suspension 31
transmission 54, 55
screw-and-locknut
valve trains 66, 67
screwdrivers 15, 39

screws 100
seals
front forks 89
two-stroke engines 73
seats, removal 35
servicing 38–95
air filter 45
brakes 48–53
cable lubrication 53
carburetor 80–1
clutch 84–5
electrical system 94–5
four-stroke engines
67–9
fuel system 46–7
hydraulic fluid 52
ignition 76–7
lubrication 40–1
maintenance chart
102–3
oil changes 42–4
spark plugs 47
special tools 62–3
steering and
suspension 60–1
suspension 86–9
tools 38–9
transmission 54–7
two-stroke engines
70–3
wheel alignment
58–9
shaft drive 54, 55
removing wheels 27
shampoo 37
shims
bucket-and-shim
valve trains 66, 68
two-stroke engines
73
shock absorbers 55, 87

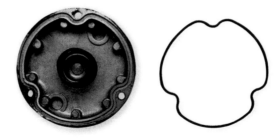

shoes, brake 51
shop manuals 38
side panels, removal 34
sight windows,
  crankcases 18
slide carburetors 78
socket sets 39
soft links, drive chains
  54, 56
soldering irons 91
spanner wrenches 63
  "C" spanner wrenches
    15, 39
  combination spanner
    wrenches 38
  open-ended spanner
    wrenches 14
  ring spanner wrenches
    15
spark plugs 47, 74, 75
  access panel 34
  spark plug adjusters
    47
  spark plug gauges 39
speedometer drive gear,
  greasing 41
split links, drive chains
  54, 56
spokes, broken 28
sponges 37
sports bikes 10
springs
  clutch 85
  suspension 30–1
sprockets, replacement
  56–7
starting problems 96–7
steering 60–1
steering-head bearings
  adjusting 61
  checking 60

greasing 41
storing bikes 37
strap wrenches 39
sump 40
  gearboxes 44
  oil change 42
suspension 30–3, 60–1
  adjustment 32–3
  greasing 41
  leaks 28
  linkage bearings 61,
    87
  maintenance chart 102
  problems 86–9
swingarm 24, 31
  bearings 60
  components 87
  greasing 41
  problems 86, 87
  removing wheels 27
switches, lubrication 41

T
tachometer cable,
  greasing 41
tap and die sets 90
  repairing threads 100
tape 91
telescopic forks 31
  components 86
  lubrication 41
  oil replacement 86
  overhaul 88–9
tensioner, camshaft 69
terminals, electrics 94,
  95
test lights 95
threads, repairing 100
throttle, cable
  lubrication 53
timing 64, 76–7

timing guns 62, 77
tools
  for cleaning 37
  for resolving problems
    90–1
  for servicing 38–9
  special tools 62–3
  toolkits 14–15
toothed-belt drive 55
torque wrenches 63
"total-loss" system
  18, 70
trail bikes 11
transmission 54–7
  automatic 13
  chain and sprocket
    replacement 56–7
  drive systems 54–5
  maintenance chart 103
tread, tires 29
tubeless tires, repairing
  99
tubes, changing tires
  98–9
two-stroke engines 11
  components 72–3
  maintenance chart 103
  oil 40, 42, 70
  oil levels 18
  operation 70–1
tire levers 90, 98
tire valve tools 90
tires
  changing 98–9
  checks 29
  maintenance chart 103

V
vacuum gauges 63,
  80–1
valve-train systems

66–8
valves
  four-stroke engines
    66, 67
  suspension 31
  two-stroke engines
    72, 73
Venturi effect 78
vernier gauges 63, 85
viscosity, oil 40

W
washers 91
washing bikes 36–7
water-repellent sprays
  36, 94
wet-sump engines
  41, 42
wheels
  alignment 58–9
  bearings 61, 99
  changing tires 98–9
  inspection 28
  lubricating bearings
    41
  maintenance chart 103
  removal 26–7
  suspension 30
  tires 29
winter, prewinter care
  37
wire-stripping tool 91
wires, repairing broken
  95
wiring diagrams see
  circuit diagrams
wrenches 14, 15, 33,
  39, 63

Acknowledgments

AUTHOR'S ACKNOWLEDGMENTS

Many people helped in the production of this book. Those who deserve special thanks are: Benji Straw and David Champion at Piaggio UK and Stephen Hartwell at Yamaha UK for knowing lots and answering my questions; Lol Henderson for again attempting to unravel the mysteries of electricity for me; Stephen Croucher and Peter Miles for reading the manuscript; Ray and Brian at Chelsea Scooters, Norman Birtles at MPS, David Fiddaman of Davida, and Stan Stephens for providing bits to photograph in a hurry.

The excellent team at DK deserve thanks, too: Sasha Kennedy put up with more than a canceled meeting; David "Thus" Walton breathed a sigh of relief; Tracy Hambleton-Miles and Louise Candlish supervised the project; Tina Vaughan and Sean Moore managed the supervisors; Simon Murrell kept his bike clean; Andy Crawford took the photos and painted his bike with the gaudiest color scheme in West London; Gary Ombler helped him.

I'd also like to thank Phil Smith for overhauling my bike while I was busy working on this book.

DK WOULD LIKE TO THANK:

Gwen Edmonds; Simon Murrell for modeling and technical advice; Stephen Croucher, Lol Henderson, and Peter Miles for technical advice; Hilary Bird for the index; Mick Gillah for his artworks; and Stephen Hartwell at Yamaha UK for so generously offering his help and his time, above and beyond the call of duty. Also, thanks go to Honda, Micron, Davida, Facom, Piaggio, Yamaha, and Rex Judd for the loan of items for photography.

PICTURE CREDITS

Additional photography:
l=left; r=right; t=top; b=bottom; c=center
pp.11, 30 (l), 47 (tr), 49 (tr, bl), 73 (bl, br), 74 (c), 75 (tl, tr, c, cr, br), 78 (br), 79 (t), 87 (l), 102 (cl), 103 (cl): Dave King

p.37 (tl): Phil Gatward

Artworks:
pp.65, 71, 92–93: Mick Gillah

pp.31, 48 (tr), 64, 70, 74, 78 (bl): Nicolas Hall

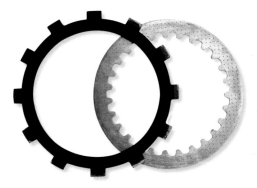